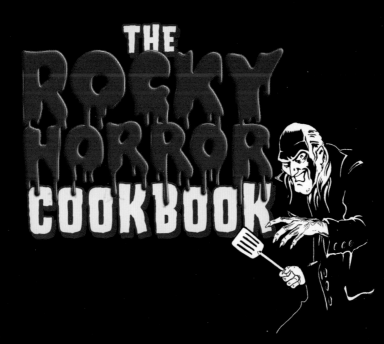

THE ROCKY HORROR COOKBOOK

50 SAVORY, SWEET, AND SEDUCTIVE RECIPES
FROM THE CULT MUSICAL

KIM LAIDLAW

FOREWORD BY RICHARD O'BRIEN

Running Press
Hachette Book Group
1290 Avenue of the Americas, New York, NY 10104
www.runningpress.com
@Running_Press

First Edition: September 2024

Published by Running Press, an imprint of Hachette
Book Group, Inc. The Running Press name and logo
are trademarks of Hachette Book Group, Inc.

The Hachette Speakers Bureau provides a wide range
of authors for speaking events. To find out more,
go to www.hachettespeakersbureau.com or email
HachetteSpeakers@hbgusa.com.

Running Press books may be purchased in bulk for
business, educational, or promotional use. For more
information, please contact your local bookseller or
the Hachette Book Group Special Markets Department
at Special.Markets@hbgusa.com.

Print book cover and interior design by
Frances J. Soo Ping Chow

Library of Congress Cataloging-in-Publication Data
Names: Laidlaw, Kim, author.
Title: The Rocky Horror cookbook : 50 savory,
  sweet, and seductive recipes from the cult musical /
  Kim Laidlaw.
Description: First edition. | Philadelphia : Running
  Press/Hachette Book Group, 2024. | Includes index. |
Summary: "Celebrate 50 years of Rocky Horror
  with this officially licensed cookbook inspired by
  the beloved cult classic musical" —Provided by
  publisher.
Identifiers: LCCN 2023041055 (print) | LCCN 2023041056
  (ebook) | ISBN 9780762487325 (hardcover) |
  ISBN 9780762487332 (ebook)
Subjects: LCSH: Cooking. | Rocky Horror picture show
  (Motion picture) |
Literary cookbooks. | LCGFT: Cookbooks.
Classification: LCC TX714 .L3365 2024 (print) |
  LCC TX714 (ebook) | DDC 641.5—dc23/eng/20231103
LC record available at https://lccn.loc.gov/2023041055
LC ebook record available at
  https://lccn.loc.gov/2023041056

ISBNs: 978-0-7624-8732-5 (hardcover),
978-0-7624-8733-2 (ebook)

Printed in China

APS

10 9 8 7 6 5 4 3 2 1

ILLUSTRATION CREDITS
cover and pp. i, x, 20, 60, 83 by Vince Ray

PHOTO CREDITS
pp. viii, 31, 48, 54, 58, 68, 77 © Everett Collection
p. xiii © Richard O'Brien
pp. 4, 43, 106 © Shutterstock
p. 17 Haley Flaherty and Richard Meek as Janet and Brad; photo © David Freeman
p. 85 Haley Flaherty as Janet; photo © David Freeman
All additional photos © Getty Images

CONTENTS

FOREWORD

by Richard O'Brien

Food can be
FUN
But more loosely fuel
Such as,
A
Warm
Loving-bowlful
When the winters are cruel
Or
A roast
Or
A grill
Or chilli on toast with a chilled
   pickled dill.

Be it
BREAKFAST
Or
SUPPER
BRUNCH
LUNCH
Or
TEA
Here are meals of appeal
   with their own recipe.
They were tested by
GHOULS

And
GROUPS
Of
DUPED-FOOLS
Who succumbed to
   the pleasures of flattery
And at the end of the
TRIAL
They all wore a smile
And each thanked us for
   charging their battery.

AND NOW
Our promise to
YOU
With our hands on our
HEARTS
Is that we are bound to confound you
   with all sorts of sauce
And
ASTOUND
ALL
You
LOVERS
Of
TARTS.

INTRODUCTION

"THAT'S HOW I DISCOVERED THE SECRET—THAT ELUSIVE INGREDIENT—THAT SPARK THAT IS THE BREATH OF LIFE."

—Dr. Frank-N-Furter

reated by actor, writer, and musician Richard O'Brien, *The Rocky Horror Show* hit the stage in 1973 at London's Royal Court Theatre Upstairs to an audience of only sixty-three people. It was an immediate success, swiftly transcending boundaries and finding a cherished place in theaters across London. The magnetic appeal of the play knew no bounds, and productions cropped up across the world in the ensuing years. The film adaptation of the musical, known as *The Rocky Horror Picture Show*, hit the screens in 1975, and initially faced critical backlash. But adoring fans of both the play and the film formed a dedicated community, often dressing up as their favorite characters and interacting with the stage characters. This unique interaction—allowing admirers to actively participate in the celebration of *The Rocky Horror Show*—played a pivotal role in sustaining its allure over the past five decades.

The play, *The Rocky Horror Show*, is a magnificent homage to the B movies, science fiction and horror films of the golden era from the 1930s to the 1960s. Infused with the essence of glam rock, the plot weaves the tale of a newly engaged (and pretty uptight)

couple whose fateful stormy night tire blowout leads them to the eerie home of mad scientist Dr. Frank-N-Furter. Along with his wild band of misfits, Frank unveils his latest creation—a muscle man named Rocky Horror—and a whirlwind of dramatic events are unleashed that captivate audiences to this day.

More than just entertaining spectacle, *The Rocky Horror Show* and *The Rocky Horror Picture Show* hold profound cultural significance, both influenced by and influencing the countercultural and sexual liberation movements that swept the 1970s and 1980s. Breaking new ground, the musical presented liberated characters, showcasing fluid sexualities at a time when such portrayals were rarely seen. Today, *The Rocky Horror Show* and its film counterpart, *The Rocky Horror Picture Show*, continue to reign as timeless cult classics, captivating audiences across the globe. Celebrated as a vivid queer art form, they champion gender fluidity and nonconformity, resonating deeply with diverse spectators who relish their campy charm and infectious tunes.

Step into the extraordinary world of *The Rocky Horror Cookbook*, where the recipes embrace the daring spirit of the iconic characters, wild plotlines, and catchy sing-along songs. Get the party started with Pelvic Thrust Pizza Sticks (page 12) and It's Alright Janet Jalapeño Poppers (page 14), or cool things down with Thrill Me Chill Me Spicy Gazpacho (page 18). Prepare to be abducted by the otherworldly flavors of Science Fiction Spicy Shrimp (page 26), leaving you longing for more extraterrestrial delights.

But the fun doesn't end there! Jump to the left and step to the right (with your hands on your hips) and serve up Time Warp Blood Orange Martinis (page 80) to your guests, or set out a tray of Sonic Transducer "Send You to Another Planet" Shooters (page 87) that will have everyone feeling like they're on a galactic adventure.

And when it's time for the main act, prepare to be mesmerized by the soy-marinated Creature of the Night Pork Tenderloin (page 42). Sink your fangs into crispy Over at the Frankenstein Place Fried Fish Fingers (page 64), or indulge in Dr. Frank-N-Furter's Hot and Spicy Chili Dogs (page 37), a flamboyant twist on the classic.

As the night deepens, treat yourself and your guests to sweet temptations that will ignite your senses. Enter a world of indulgence with Midnight Double Chocolate Feature Brownies (page 94), a devilishly rich treat that's worth staying up for, or let the Red Lips Red Velvet Cupcakes with Red Sparkle Sugar (page 98) give you the last kiss of the night.

Get ready for a tantalizing culinary extravaganza that's as unforgettable as *The Rocky Horror Show* itself! With these daring recipes in hand, your kitchen will become a hotbed of sultry surprises and seductive flavors that'll leave you craving more. Let the cooking adventures begin—it's time to let loose and unleash your inner culinary diva!

LET'S
GET THIS
PARTY
STARTED

LATE-NIGHT

DOUBLE FEATURE

POPCORN

It's impossible to imagine SEEING A MOVIE—MUCH LESS A LATE-NIGHT DOUBLE FEATURE—WITHOUT A TUB OF POPCORN. AND POPCORN IS JUST AS FITTING FOR A THEATRICAL MUSICAL HONORING SCIENCE FICTION AND "B" HORROR FILMS (B MOVIES HAVING HISTORICALLY BEEN SHOWN AS THE COMPANION TO THE MAIN ATTRACTION IN A DOUBLE FEATURE). THIS SAVORY TREAT KICKS IT UP A NOTCH—THINK HIGH HEELS AND FISHNETS—WITH THE ADDITION OF CHILI-LIME SEASONING, BUT YOU COULD SUBSTITUTE ANY SAVORY SPICE BLEND YOU LIKE (SEE TIP).

Makes 4 to 6 servings

3 tablespoons unsalted butter

1 tablespoon chili-lime seasoning

3 tablespoons neutral oil
(such as avocado or canola)

½ cup unpopped popcorn kernels

Fine sea salt

In a small microwave-safe bowl, combine the butter and chili-lime seasoning. Melt the butter in the microwave in short bursts of 30 seconds. Stir to combine and set aside.

In a large, heavy pot over medium heat, warm the neutral oil. Add two popcorn kernels, cover, and cook until you hear the kernels pop. Remove from the heat and add the remaining kernels; swirl the pan for about 30 seconds. Re-cover the pot and continue to cook over medium heat, shaking the pan continuously, until the popping slows to 3 to 5 seconds between pops. Remove the pan from the heat and let sit for 30 seconds. Carefully lift the lid. You can also use plain microwave popcorn; you'll need about 14 cups of popped popcorn. Pour the popcorn into a serving bowl.

While the popcorn is hot, drizzle with the reserved chili-lime butter and toss to coat evenly. Season with salt and serve right away.

TIP: *Don't have chili-lime seasoning? Try 1 tablespoon chili powder mixed with 2 teaspoons finely grated lime zest instead.*

MAGENTA MINI MASH(ED) POTATO CAKES

You'll smack your sexy red lips FOR THESE SAVORY-SWEET, BITE-SIZE, FULLY LOADED POTATO CAKES. MADE WITH PURPLE SWEET POTATOES, WHICH GIVES THEM A MAGENTA HUE, THEY ARE THE IDEAL TRIBUTE TO THE SHAMELESSLY PROVOCATIVE MAGENTA, WHO ALSO HAS QUITE A BITE. IF YOU CAN'T LOCATE PURPLE SWEET POTATOES (THEY MIGHT BE FROM ANOTHER PLANET), SUBSTITUTE ORANGE-FLESHED SWEET POTATOES.

Makes about 34 mini cakes

1 medium purple sweet potato
(about 12 ounces)

2 thick-cut bacon slices
(about 2½ ounces), finely chopped

2 large eggs, beaten

¼ cup plain yogurt or sour cream,
plus more for serving

¼ cup whole milk

2 tablespoons unsalted butter, melted,
plus 1 tablespoon

½ teaspoon fine sea salt

¼ teaspoon freshly ground
black pepper

2 ounces shredded cheddar cheese

1 tablespoon finely chopped fresh
chives, plus more for garnish

½ cup all-purpose flour

½ teaspoon baking powder

¼ teaspoon baking soda

Olive oil, for cooking

Preheat the oven to 375°F.

Scrub the sweet potato, then poke it all over using a sharp paring knife. Place the sweet potato on a small baking sheet and bake until very soft, about 45 minutes. When cool enough to handle, scoop the sweet potato flesh into a bowl and mash it with a fork or potato masher until smooth. You should have 1 cup.

While the sweet potato cooks, in a skillet over medium-low heat, cook the bacon, stirring until crisp and browned, about 4 minutes. Using a slotted spoon, transfer the bacon to paper towels to drain.

Reduce the oven temperature to 200°F and place a baking sheet in the oven.

To the bowl with the sweet potatoes, add the eggs, yogurt, milk, 2 tablespoons of melted butter, salt, and pepper and stir to combine. Stir in the bacon, cheddar cheese, and chives. Add the flour, baking powder, and baking soda and stir until combined.

In a large nonstick skillet over medium heat, combine 1½ teaspoons of the remaining butter and a drizzle of olive oil and let them melt together.

For each cake, spoon 1 tablespoon of batter into the skillet, keeping the cakes separate (do not overcrowd the pan). Cook until the bottom is golden brown, about 3 minutes, then flip and cook until browned on the other side and cooked through, about 3 minutes more. If the cakes are browning too quickly, reduce the heat to medium-low. Transfer the cooked cakes to the baking sheet in the oven to keep warm while you cook the remaining cakes.

Serve warm with a dollop of yogurt, garnished with chives.

I REALLY LOVE THAT ROCK AND ROLL(S)

A battered Eddie, former delivery boy AND LOVER OF COLUMBIA, BURSTS OUT OF A LARGE CONTAINER RESEMBLING A VINTAGE REFRIGERATOR, DRESSED IN HIS 1950S ROCK-AND-ROLL LEATHER JACKET. HE BELTS OUT, "I REALLY LOVE THAT ROCK AND ROLL," WHILE COLUMBIA AND THE REST OF THE CAST GYRATE AROUND HIM. IT DOESN'T TAKE HALF A BRAIN TO MAKE THESE GARLICKY HERB–CHEDDAR ROLLS, WHICH ARE FITTING FOR ANY OCCASION, ROCK-AND-ROLL REUNION OR OTHERWISE.

Makes 15 rolls

9 tablespoons unsalted butter, plus more for the baking dish

1 cup whole milk

1 envelope (2¼ teaspoons) instant yeast

3 cups plus 2 tablespoons (14 ounces) all-purpose flour, plus more for dusting

1 large egg, lightly beaten

1½ teaspoons fine sea salt

1 tablespoon each minced fresh parsley and dill

3 ounces shredded cheddar cheese

½ teaspoon garlic powder

In a small saucepan over low heat, melt 6 tablespoons of butter. Stir in the milk and warm the mixture to about 110°F. Pour the milk mixture into the bowl of a stand mixer (or a large bowl) and whisk the yeast into the milk mixture. Let stand until foamy, about 10 minutes.

Add the flour, attach a dough hook, and mix on low speed just until the dough starts to come together. Add the egg, salt, and 1 tablespoon of the herbs. Mix on medium speed until the dough is soft and slightly sticky, about 5 minutes. Add the cheddar cheese and mix on low speed to combine. Alternatively, mix the dough in a large bowl, using a wooden spoon, then lightly dust a work surface with flour and knead the dough by hand on it.

Shape the dough into a ball, cover the bowl with plastic wrap, and let rise in a warm, draft-free spot until doubled, about 1 hour.

Generously coat a 9 by 13-inch baking dish with butter. Lightly dust a work surface with flour and transfer the dough to it. Divide the dough into 15 equal pieces, each about 2 ounces. Roll each piece into a ball and place the balls into the prepared baking dish, spacing them evenly in three rows of five. Cover loosely with plastic wrap and let stand until puffy, about 1 hour.

Preheat the oven to 375°F.

In a small microwave-safe bowl, melt the remaining 3 tablespoons of butter. Stir in the garlic powder and remaining herbs. Brush the dough balls with the butter mixture.

Bake until the rolls are puffed and golden, about 20 minutes. Serve warm.

I'M GOING HOME
HUMMUS WITH
SPICY PITA CHIPS

In a sentimental moment AT THE END OF THE SHOW, FRANK BELIEVES HE WILL RETURN HOME TO THE GALAXY OF TRANSYLVANIA—"I'VE SEEN BLUE SKIES, THROUGH THE TEARS IN MY EYES, AND I REALIZE—I'M GOING HOME . . ." BUT RIFF RAFF AND MAGENTA CAN NEVER ALLOW THAT, AND SO FRANK IS ELIMINATED. BECAUSE YOU'RE NOT FROM ANOTHER PLANET (OR A THREAT TO SOCIETY), YOU CAN GO HOME AND MAKE THIS SILKY-SMOOTH HUMMUS WITH CRUNCHY PITA CHIPS PERFECT FOR DIPPING.

Makes 6 servings

Hummus

1 (15-ounce) can chickpeas, drained and rinsed

⅓ cup tahini

⅓ cup water, plus more as needed

3 tablespoons fresh lemon juice, plus more as needed

2 tablespoons extra-virgin olive oil

2 small garlic cloves, chopped

½ teaspoon fine sea salt, plus more as needed

Pita Chips

2 pita breads (each about 7 inches in diameter)

2 tablespoons extra-virgin olive oil

2 teaspoons za'atar

1 teaspoon hot paprika

To make the hummus, combine all the hummus ingredients in a blender. Blend on high speed, stopping to scrape down the sides of the blender jar once or twice, until very smooth. If needed, add more water, 1 tablespoon at a time, to reach the consistency you desire (the hummus will thicken slightly once chilled). Taste and season with more salt or lemon juice, if you like. Transfer to a bowl and set aside. The hummus, about 2 cups, can be refrigerated in an airtight container for up to 1 week.

Preheat the oven to 350°F.

To make the pita chips, split each pita bread horizontally into 2 thin rounds. In a small bowl, stir together the olive oil and spices. Stack the pita rounds and cut them like a cake into 6 wedges (for a total of 24 wedges). Brush the wedges on one side with the oil-spice mixture. Transfer the wedges to a baking sheet, oil side up, and bake until crisp and golden, 10 to 15 minutes depending on the thickness of the pitas. Transfer the baking sheet to a wire rack and let cool; the chips will crisp as they cool.

Serve chips alongside the hummus.

The Phantoms are minor CHARACTERS WHO APPEAR IN THE EARLY PART OF THE PLAY, AND ALSO SERVE AS THE BACKUP CHORUS, "OOHING" AND "JANET-ING" IN THE BACKGROUND. OOHING AND AAHING MIGHT HAPPEN WHEN YOU MAKE THESE VERSATILE BITE-SIZE FRITTATAS, IDEAL FOR SNACKING ANY TIME OF DAY OR DURING ANY PART OF THE SHOW.

Makes 12 bites; 4 servings

3 ounces fresh baby spinach

Cooking spray, for the pan

3 large eggs

1 tablespoon whole milk

½ teaspoon minced fresh thyme or oregano leaves, chives, or a mixture

Fine sea salt and freshly ground black pepper

About 1 ounce crumbled feta cheese

Preheat the oven to 350°F.

Fill a medium bowl with ice water. Bring a saucepan half full of salted water to a boil over high heat. Add the spinach and cook, stirring, just until wilted, about 30 seconds. Immediately drain the spinach, then plunge it into the ice water to stop the cooking. When cool, drain the spinach (removing any ice), and squeeze out the excess water with your hands. Transfer to a cutting board. Use paper towels to pat the spinach as dry as possible, then chop the spinach finely.

Generously coat 12 cups of a mini muffin pan with cooking spray, or line them with foil liners. In a medium bowl, whisk together the eggs, milk, herbs, and chopped spinach. Season with salt and pepper to taste. Divide the egg mixture evenly among the prepared muffin cups, filling them nearly full. Sprinkle each with a bit of feta.

Bake until set and the edges are browned, about 15 minutes. Transfer the pan to a wire rack and let cool for 5 minutes. Use a small knife to help release the mini frittatas from the cups. Serve warm.

The frittatas can be refrigerated in an airtight container for up to 3 days, or frozen for up to 3 months.

TIP: *To mix things up, instead of spinach, use ¼ cup finely chopped cooked veggies, such as mushrooms, asparagus, broccoli, red bell pepper, or a mixture, and swap shredded cheddar for the feta.*

PHANTOM
FRITTATA BITES

PELVIC THRUST PIZZA STICKS

The energetic dance moves—most NOTABLY THE INFAMOUS PELVIC THRUSTS— OF "THE TIME WARP" WILL LEAVE YOU FAMISHED. SAVOR THESE CHEESY PIZZA STICKS TOPPED WITH TANGY SAUCE AND YOUR FAVORITE TOPPINGS. IT'S EASIER TO CUT THESE INTO STICKS IF THE TOPPINGS ARE CUT INTO SMALL PIECES. AND DON'T OVERLOAD YOUR PIZZAS, OR YOUR DANCE MOVES.

Makes 6 to 8 servings

1 pound store-bought pizza dough

Olive oil, for brushing

½ cup pizza sauce

About 7 ounces shredded mozzarella cheese

About ½ cup chopped pizza toppings (such as pepperoni, chopped cooked bacon, sautéed mushrooms, sliced black or green olives, ham, pineapple, halved cherry tomatoes, etc.)

Let the dough sit out at room temperature for at least 1 hour before starting.

Position an oven rack in the center of the oven and preheat to 475°F. Line two large, rimmed baking sheets with parchment paper and brush generously with olive oil.

Divide the pizza dough in half. Place one half of the pizza dough on one of the prepared baking sheets and stretch and pull it into a large rectangle of even thickness, about 6 by 17 inches. (Picking up the dough and letting gravity help stretch it works well!)

Spread half of the pizza sauce over the pizza dough, leaving a ¼- to ½-inch border (do not slop it over the edge; it will burn and stick). Sprinkle half the mozzarella evenly over the sauce. Arrange half the toppings evenly on top.

Bake the pizza until the cheese is bubbly and the crust is golden, 15 to 18 minutes. Transfer to a wire rack to cool for a couple of minutes, then slide the pizza onto a cutting board. Using a pizza cutter or a large knife, cut crosswise into "sticks." Serve at once.

Repeat to make and bake the remaining pizza.

IT'S ALRIGHT JANET

JALAPEÑO POPPERS

Brad repeatedly comforts Janet BY UTTERING, "IT'S ALRIGHT JANET," WHILE THE COUPLE NAVIGATES THE BIZARRE AND THRILLING JOURNEY THAT IS *ROCKY HORROR*. THE SPICY HEAT OF THESE BAKED JALAPEÑO POPPERS MOMENTARILY IGNITES A THRILL BEFORE THE CREAMINESS OF THE CHEESE SOOTHES AND COMFORTS. OMIT THE BACON TO KEEP THESE VEGETARIAN.

Makes 6 to 8 servings

2 thick-cut smoked bacon slices (about 2½ ounces), finely chopped

⅓ cup panko breadcrumbs

⅓ cup grated Parmesan cheese, plus ¼ cup

½ teaspoon smoked paprika (optional)

8 ounces cream cheese, at room temperature

2 ounces shredded cheddar cheese

2 small green onions, white and green parts, minced

12 medium jalapeño chiles

In a skillet over medium heat, cook the bacon, stirring occasionally, until golden, about 5 minutes. Using a slotted spoon, transfer the bacon to paper towels to drain. Let cool.

In a shallow bowl, stir together the panko, ⅓ cup of Parmesan, and the paprika (if using).

In a medium bowl, stir together the cream cheese, cheddar, remaining ¼ cup of Parmesan, reserved bacon, and the green onions until well combined.

Preheat the oven to 400°F.

Halve the jalapeños lengthwise, then use a teaspoon to scoop out and discard the seeds (it's recommended to wear rubber gloves when working with chiles). Arrange the jalapeño halves, cut side up, on a rimmed baking sheet.

Divide the cream cheese filling among the jalapeño halves, then press the cheese-filled side of each jalapeño in the panko mixture, pressing the mixture into the cheese. Arrange the jalapeño halves on the baking sheet, stuffed side up.

Bake until bubbling and golden brown, about 15 minutes. If you like, turn on the broiler, then slide the baking sheet under the broiler to toast the filling a bit more. (Use a small spatula or butter knife to push any filling that bubbles out back into the jalapeño.) Let sit for 5 minutes, then serve warm.

LASER BEAM BAKED
BACON-WRAPPED DATES

Great heavens! Although these BACON-WRAPPED DATES MIGHT NOT POSSESS THE POWER TO UNLEASH A BEAM OF PURE ANTI-MATTER, THEY WILL UNDOUBTEDLY SATISFY YOUR EARTHLY CRAVINGS. BRACE YOURSELF FOR AN EXPLOSION OF SAVORY CHEESE AND CARAMELIZED BACON, PERFECTLY COMPLEMENTING THE SOFT, MOLASSES-SWEET DATES. IT'S A TASTE SENSATION THAT MIGHT JUST BLOW YOU OUT OF THIS WORLD.

Makes 4 to 6 servings

12 large Medjool dates

2½ to 3 ounces crumbled blue cheese or goat cheese

6 thin bacon slices, halved crosswise

2 tablespoons maple syrup

½ teaspoon minced fresh rosemary leaves

Freshly ground black pepper

Preheat the oven to 400°F. Line a small, rimmed baking sheet with parchment paper or aluminum foil.

Cut each date lengthwise down one side—do not cut all the way through—and remove the pit. Stuff each date with blue cheese and press the halves together. Wrap a half bacon slice around each date and secure with a toothpick. Arrange the dates on the prepared baking sheet.

In a small bowl, stir together the maple syrup, rosemary, and a few grinds of pepper.

Bake the dates until the bacon fat renders and the bacon starts to crisp, 15 to 20 minutes, turning once halfway through. Brush the dates on both sides with the maple syrup mixture. Continue baking until the bacon is caramelized but not burnt, turning once, about 5 minutes longer. The dates will be plump and lustful. Let cool for at least 5 minutes before serving.

JANET AND BRAD'S UNDRESSED SALAD CAPRESE

Like Janet and Brad, THIS STRIPPED-DOWN VERSION OF A "NAKED" CAPRESE SALAD IS NOTHING LESS THAN ALLURING. A VIBRANT COMBINATION OF SUN-KISSED SUMMER TOMATOES, EARTHY BASIL, AND CREAMY MOZZARELLA CREATES A TANTALIZING FEAST FOR THE SENSES. EAT IT FULLY CLOTHED OR JUST IN YOUR KNICKERS, IF YOU LIKE.

Makes 4 to 6 servings

2 pounds mixed ripe fresh tomatoes (such as heirloom and cherry tomatoes)

1 pound fresh mozzarella cheese, drained and sliced or cut into chunks

Fine sea salt and freshly ground black pepper

¼ cup basil pesto, at room temperature

Extra-virgin olive oil and balsamic vinegar, for drizzling

Handful of baby arugula

Cut the tomatoes into slices or chunks; if using cherry or grape tomatoes, halve them. Arrange the mozzarella slices and tomatoes on a large platter. Season with salt and pepper.

Drizzle the pesto over the tomatoes and mozzarella (if the pesto is thick, add a little oil or water to loosen it), then drizzle with a little olive oil and balsamic vinegar. Garnish with the arugula for a sexy spicy kick, and serve at once.

THRILL ME CHILL ME SPICY GAZPACHO

With its refreshing blend OF FLAVORS, THIS CHILLED GAZPACHO WILL THRILL YOU AND FULFILL YOU, MUCH LIKE THE CREATURE OF THE NIGHT. IT'S BEST MADE WHEN FRESH TOMATOES AND CUCUMBERS ARE AT THE PEAK OF THEIR SUMMER SEASON. TO SEED TOMATOES, TAKE THOSE PLUMP, JUICY GEMS AND SLICE THEM CROSSWISE WITH A DEVILISH GRIN. TOUCH-A TOUCH-A TOUCH THE TOMATOES GENTLY, WHILE SQUEEZING THE SEEDS INTO A FINE-MESH SIEVE SET OVER A BOWL TO CAPTURE THE JUICES.

Makes 6 servings

3 pounds ripe fresh heirloom tomatoes, seeded and roughly chopped, plus more for garnish

1 cup drained and chopped roasted red peppers (such as piquillo peppers)

6-inch-long English cucumber, chopped

¼ cup extra-virgin olive oil, plus more for drizzling

2 tablespoons hot pepper sauce, plus more as needed

1 tablespoon Worcestershire sauce

1 tablespoon white wine vinegar, plus more as needed

Fine sea salt and freshly ground black pepper

Cubed avocado, diced cucumber, and/or croutons, for garnish

Fresh herbs, such as cilantro and thyme, for garnish

In a blender, combine the tomatoes, red peppers, cucumber, olive oil, hot sauce, Worcestershire sauce, and vinegar, being careful to fill your blender only three-fourths full. (Halve the ingredients if you need to do this in batches). Puree on high speed until very smooth. Season to taste with salt and pepper, and adjust the hot sauce and vinegar to your liking.

Strain the soup through a fine-mesh sieve over a large bowl, using a rubber spatula to push the soup through the sieve. Transfer to an airtight container and chill for at least 1 hour.

To serve, ladle the soup into bowls and garnish each serving with tomato, avocado, cucumber, croutons, and/or fresh herbs. Drizzle seductively with a little olive oil.

HOT PATOOTIE POTATO LEEK SOUP

Sharp-dressing Eddie might be HALF-DEAD, BUT IT DOESN'T STOP HIM FROM BELTING OUT A LAMENT TO HIS FORMER LUSTY SATURDAY NIGHTS WITH GIRLFRIEND COLUMBIA. "HOT PATOOTIE BLESS [YOUR] SOUL" BY MAKING THIS SILKY-SMOOTH POTATO LEEK SOUP, A PERFECT WAY TO START YOUR SATURDAY NIGHT MEAL. TO MAKE IT VEGAN, USE 4½ CUPS VEGETABLE STOCK, OMIT THE HEAVY CREAM, AND USE OLIVE OIL INSTEAD OF BUTTER.

Makes 4 to 6 servings

2 tablespoons unsalted butter

2 large leeks, white and pale green parts, halved lengthwise, rinsed well, and sliced (about 4 cups)

Fine sea salt and freshly ground black pepper

2 russet potatoes (about 1¼ pounds), peeled and cut into 1-inch pieces

4 cups good-quality low-sodium chicken stock, plus more as needed

½ cup heavy cream

Minced fresh chives, for serving (optional)

In a large saucepan over medium-low heat, melt the butter. Add the leeks and a pinch of salt and cook, stirring, until very tender but not browned, about 12 minutes. Add the potatoes and stock and season with salt and pepper. Increase the heat to medium-high and bring to a boil. Reduce the heat to medium-low, cover the pan, and simmer, stirring occasionally, until the potatoes are very tender, 15 to 20 minutes.

Stir in the heavy cream.

Working in batches, if necessary, transfer the soup to a blender. Blend, starting on low speed and increasing the speed slowly to medium-high, until the soup is silky smooth. (Be careful not to blend the soup too long or the potatoes might become gluey.) Return the soup to the saucepan. Add more stock, if needed, to get to the consistency you like. Warm the soup gently over medium-low heat until hot.

Season to taste with salt and pepper, then ladle into soup bowls and garnish with chives (if using) to serve.

FRANK'S FRIGHTFUL FRENCH ONION SOUP

Mad scientist Frank-N-Furter is obsessed WITH CREATING THE PERFECT LIFE FORM AS HIS SEXUAL PLAYTHING. HIS ECCENTRIC BEHAVIOR IS BOTH FRIGHTFUL AND DELIGHTFUL AS HE STRUTS ACROSS THE STAGE IN HIS CASTLE AND LABORATORY. THIS FRENCH ONION SOUP, WITH ITS SWEET, CARAMELIZED ONIONS, FLAVORFUL BROTH, AND MELTY CHEESE-TOPPED TOASTS, IS PERFECTLY DELIGHTFUL, NEVER FRIGHTFUL. CREATE IT IN YOUR KITCHEN LABORATORY, AND LEAVE THE LIFE FORMS TO FRANK.

Makes 6 servings

4 large yellow onions (about 3 pounds)

3 tablespoons extra-virgin olive oil

Fine sea salt and freshly ground black pepper

2 tablespoons unsalted butter

1 teaspoon sugar

½ cup dry white wine

2 tablespoons dry sherry

2 thyme sprigs, plus thyme leaves for garnish

6 cups good-quality beef, chicken, or mushroom stock

6 large, thick slices French bread

1½ cups grated Gruyère cheese

Peel, halve, and slice the onions thinly. In a large, heavy pot or Dutch oven over medium heat, warm 2 tablespoons of olive oil. Add the onions, season with salt and pepper, and stir to combine. Cover the pot and reduce the heat to medium-low. Cook, stirring occasionally, until the onions soften and start to brown, about 15 minutes. Add the butter, stir until melted, then re-cover the pot and continue to cook, stirring often, until the onions are caramelized, about 25 minutes longer; during the last 5 minutes of cooking, remove the lid. Stir in the sugar and cook, uncovered and stirring, for 3 minutes.

Increase the heat to medium and add the wine, sherry, and thyme. Stir, scraping any browned bits from the bottom of the pot. Bring to a boil and cook until the wine evaporates, about 2 minutes. Stir in the stock and bring to a gentle boil, then adjust the heat to maintain a gentle simmer and let cook for about 15 minutes to bring the flavors together.

Meanwhile, make the cheese toasts. Position an oven rack in the upper-third of the oven and preheat the oven to 450°F.

Brush both sides of each bread slice with the remaining 1 tablespoon of olive oil, then arrange them on a large baking sheet. Bake, turning once, until nicely toasted, about 6 minutes. Remove from the oven and top each toast with Gruyère, dividing evenly. Just before serving, turn the oven to broil and pop the baking sheet under the broiler to melt the cheese.

To serve, remove and discard the thyme sprigs and ladle the soup into bowls. Top each serving with a cheese toast, garnish with some fresh thyme, and serve right away.

DON'T DREAM IT,
BE(AT) IT
CHEESE SOUFFLÉ

"Give yourself over to ABSOLUTE PLEASURE . . ." BY MAKING THIS OTHERWORLDLY CHEESE SOUFFLÉ. DON'T [JUST] DREAM [ABOUT] IT, BE IT! IT'S EASIER THAN YOU MAY THINK TO WHIP UP. USE ANY OF YOUR FAVORITE MELTING CHEESES, OR A BLEND. AND BE SURE YOUR AUDIENCE IS CAPTIVE AND READY TO EAT. A SOUFFLÉ WAITS FOR NO ONE.

Makes 6 soufflés

3 tablespoons unsalted butter, plus more for the ramekins

Finely grated Parmesan cheese, for the ramekins

3 tablespoons all-purpose flour

1½ cups whole milk

6 ounces shredded cheddar or Gruyère cheese, or a combination

Fine sea salt and freshly ground black pepper

4 large eggs, separated, plus 1 large egg white

½ teaspoon cream of tartar

1 tablespoon minced fresh chives

Position an oven rack in the lower third of the oven and preheat the oven to 400°F. Generously coat six 1-cup ramekins with butter, then lightly coat with Parmesan. Place the ramekins on a baking sheet.

In a saucepan over medium heat, melt the butter, then whisk in the flour. Cook, whisking constantly, for 2 minutes. While whisking constantly, slowly pour in the milk and bring to a boil. Reduce the heat to low and simmer gently, stirring, until the mixture thickens, about 3 minutes.

Sprinkle in the cheddar, stirring gently until melted and smooth. Taste and season with salt and pepper.

In a large bowl, whisk together the egg yolks. Slowly pour the cheese sauce into the yolks, whisking constantly.

In the bowl of a stand mixer fitted with the whisk attachment, beat the 5 egg whites and cream of tartar to thick, stiff peaks. Do not overbeat. (Alternatively, use another large bowl and a handheld electric mixer.) Stir about one-fourth of the whipped egg whites into the cheese mixture. Fold in the remaining whipped egg whites and the chives gently. Divide the batter among the prepared ramekins; they should be nearly full.

Bake until the soufflés are puffed and browned but the center still jiggles slightly when the dish is shaken gently, about 20 minutes. Do not open the oven door while the soufflés are baking.

Serve at once while hot, hot, hot.

SCIENCE FICTION SPICY SHRIMP

A spellbinding blend of SCIENCE FICTION AND MUSICAL THEATER, *ROCKY HORROR* CAPTIVATES AUDIENCES WITH ITS UNIQUE FLAVORS—KIND OF LIKE THE FIERY FLAVORS OF THIS GRILLED SHRIMP, ALWAYS LEAVING YOU WANTING MORE. SERVE THESE SPICY SHRIMP ON THEIR OWN, OR SERVE THEM OVER A BOWL OF RICE WITH LIGHTLY GRILLED BOK CHOY.

Makes 4 to 6 servings

32 medium shrimp, peeled and deveined, with tails on

Olive oil, for brushing

Fine sea salt

2 tablespoons chili crisp, plus more as needed

1 lime, halved

2 tablespoons chopped fresh cilantro

Sweet red chili sauce, for serving (optional)

Soak 8 bamboo skewers in cold water for at least 30 minutes.

Prepare a charcoal or gas grill for direct-heat grilling over medium-high heat. Brush the grill grates clean.

Thread 4 shrimp onto each of the soaked skewers. Brush the shrimp with olive oil, then season with salt.

Grill the shrimp until nicely charred on one side, about 1 minute. Turn and brush the grill-marked side with the chili crisp. Continue to grill the shrimp until they are opaque, 1 to 2 minutes longer, being careful not to overcook them. Transfer to a platter, squeeze a lime half over the shrimp and brush with additional chili crisp if you like a bit more seductive spice.

Cut the remaining lime half into wedges. Garnish the shrimp with the cilantro and serve at once with lime wedges for squeezing and chili sauce, if using.

COLUMBIA'S CHICKEN EMPANADAS

COLUMBIA'S CHICKEN EMPANADAS

Columbia, groupie and ex-lover TO THE MADMAN FRANK AS WELL AS EX-GIRLFRIEND TO THE NOW-DECEASED EDDIE, IS PASSIONATE ABOUT HER LOVES AND HER SORROWS. PASSION IS A KEY INGREDIENT TO MAKING THESE SAVORY EMPANADAS, STUFFED WITH A MIXTURE OF CHICKEN, CHORIZO, AND OLIVES. MAKE THESE AS BIG OR SMALL AS YOU LIKE, AND IF MAKING YOUR OWN DOUGH CAUSES SORROW, JUST USE STORE-BOUGHT PIE DOUGH OR PUFF PASTRY; BAKING TIMES MIGHT VARY.

Makes 8 empanadas

DOUGH

2¼ cups unbleached all-purpose flour, plus more for dusting

8 tablespoons (1 stick) cold unsalted butter, diced

1 teaspoon fine sea salt

1 large egg

2 tablespoons ice-cold water

1 tablespoon distilled white vinegar

CHICKEN FILLING

1 tablespoon extra-virgin olive oil

½ small yellow onion, finely chopped

1 large garlic clove, minced

¼ cup finely diced Spanish chorizo

¼ teaspoon smoked paprika

2 tablespoons dry white wine or reduced-sodium chicken broth

5 ounces finely chopped or shredded cooked chicken (about ¾ cup)

2 tablespoons finely chopped pitted green olives (such as Castelvetrano)

Fine sea salt and freshly ground black pepper

1 large egg beaten with 1 teaspoon water

2 ounces shredded Monterey Jack cheese

To make the dough, in the bowl of a food processor, combine the flour, butter, and salt. Process just until the mixture looks like fresh breadcrumbs. In a large bowl, whisk together the egg, cold water, and vinegar until blended. Add the flour mixture and stir together with a fork. Press the dough together into a disk and wrap tightly in plastic wrap. Refrigerate for at least 30 minutes, or up to 1 day, before using, or freeze for up to 1 month.

To make the filling, in a small skillet over medium-low heat, warm the olive oil. Cook the onion, stirring, until tender and golden, about 10 minutes. Add the garlic and sauté until fragrant, about 1 minute. Add the chorizo and paprika and cook, stirring, until the chorizo is heated through, 1 to 2 minutes. Pour in the wine, stirring until it is nearly evaporated, then stir in the chicken and olives. Season to taste with salt and pepper. Set aside to cool completely. The filling can be made up to 3 days in advance; refrigerate in an airtight container.

Lightly dust a work surface with flour, then roll out the dough on it into a round about ⅛ inch thick. Use an inverted 5-inch-diameter bowl to cut out rounds of dough. Press the dough scraps together and re-roll them to cut out more rounds until you have 8 rounds of dough. Line a large, rimmed baking sheet with parchment paper. Arrange the dough rounds on the prepared baking sheet and refrigerate until chilled.

Preheat the oven to 375°F.

To assemble the empanadas, lay the dough rounds on a work surface. Brush one half of each dough round with the egg wash. Divide the filling evenly among the dough rounds, mounding it in the center of each round. Top each with a large pinch of cheese, dividing it evenly. Pick up each dough round like a taco and press the edges together firmly while holding the filling in the center, pressing out any air from within.

Arrange the empanadas on the prepared baking sheet. Use a fork to crimp the edges of each empanada, sealing it completely. Poke holes in the top of the empanadas to let steam vent. Brush each empanada with egg wash.

Bake until golden brown, 25 to 30 minutes. Let rest for 10 minutes, then devour.

"BIT OF A MIND FLIP" MEAT LOAF

Although Eddie was originally played BY PADDY O'HAGAN IN THE 1973 LONDON CAST, MEAT LOAF PLAYED HIS CHARACTER IN THE LOS ANGELES ROXY CAST IN 1974. IT'S ALL "A BIT OF A MIND FLIP [WHEN] YOU'RE THERE IN THE TIME SLIP." THIS UPDATED MEAT LOAF IS WORTH FLIPPING OVER— A SPICED, TANGY-SWEET TOMATO CHUTNEY FLAVORS THE MEAT AND BLANKETS THE LOAF, ENSURING IT STAYS TENDER.

Makes 6 to 8 servings

TOMATO CHUTNEY

2 tablespoons olive oil

1 teaspoon whole yellow mustard seeds

½ yellow onion, finely chopped

2 garlic cloves, minced

⅓ cup packed light brown sugar

¼ cup apple cider vinegar

½ teaspoon ground cinnamon

½ teaspoon ground ginger

Fine sea salt

1 (14.5-ounce) can crushed tomatoes

1 teaspoon fresh lemon juice

Chopped fresh flat-leaf parsley, for garnish (optional)

MEAT LOAF

Cooking spray, for the baking sheet

1 cup fresh white breadcrumbs (about 3 ounces)

½ cup whole milk

3 large eggs, beaten

1 medium yellow onion, finely chopped

1½ teaspoons fine sea salt

1 teaspoon ground cumin

½ teaspoon ground coriander

½ teaspoon freshly ground black pepper

2 pounds ground beef or dark-meat turkey

To make the tomato chutney, in a saucepan over medium-low heat, warm the olive oil. Add the mustard seeds, then the onion and garlic. Cook, stirring often, until the onion softens, about 5 minutes. Stir in the brown sugar, vinegar, cinnamon, ginger, and 1 teaspoon of salt. Add the tomatoes. Simmer, stirring, until the mixture thickens, about 15 minutes. Remove from the heat and stir in the lemon juice. Set aside to cool completely. The chutney can be made up to 1 week in advance; refrigerate in an airtight container.

To make the meat loaf, position an oven rack in the upper third of the oven and preheat the oven to 400°F. Line a rimmed baking sheet with parchment paper and spray the parchment lightly with cooking spray.

In a large bowl, stir together the bread-crumbs and milk. Add ¼ cup of chutney, the eggs, onion, salt, cumin, coriander, and pepper. Stir well to combine, then crumble the meat into the mixture and stir gently to combine. Transfer the mixture to the prepared baking sheet and press it into a log about 12 inches long and 5 inches wide.

Bake for 30 minutes.

Spread ½ cup of chutney over the top and sides of the meat loaf. Return it to the oven and bake until an instant-read thermometer inserted in the center registers 165°F, 15 to 20 minutes.

Let rest for about 5 minutes before cutting into thick, hunky slices. Serve warm, garnished with the parsley (if using), and the remaining chutney alongside.

"With a bit of a mind flip ... you're there in the time slip."

DR. FRANK-N-FURTER'S HOT AND SPICY CHILI DOGS

"Flamboyant" and "indulgent" are words THAT EQUALLY DESCRIBE BOTH FRANK-N-FURTER AND THESE HOT AND SPICY CHILI DOGS (I.E., FRANKFURTERS). THEIR FIERY ESSENCE MATCHES FRANK'S DARING PERSONA AND FLAIR FOR EXTRAVAGANCE—TRULY A DELIGHT TO DEVOUR. THE CHILI IS ALSO TERRIFIC ON ITS OWN IF YOU'VE HAD ENOUGH FRANK-N-FURTERS FOR ONE NIGHT.

Makes 8 chili dogs

CHILI

1 tablespoon canola oil

½ small yellow onion, finely chopped

Fine sea salt and freshly ground black pepper

1 pound ground chuck or sirloin

2 tablespoons chili powder

1 teaspoon ground cumin

½ teaspoon garlic powder

½ teaspoon cayenne pepper, plus more as needed

¾ cup canned crushed tomatoes

¼ cup ketchup

1 tablespoon Dijon mustard

8 all-beef hot dogs

8 hot dog buns

Grated cheddar cheese and chopped red onion, for serving

To make the chili, in a heavy saucepan or Dutch oven over medium heat, warm the canola oil. Add the yellow onion and a pinch of salt and cook, stirring, until the onion softens and starts to brown, about 5 minutes.

Increase the heat to medium-high. Add the ground beef and cook, stirring, until no longer pink, about 5 minutes.

Stir in the chili powder, cumin, garlic powder, cayenne, ½ teaspoon of salt, and ½ teaspoon of pepper until combined. Stir in the tomatoes, ketchup, and mustard. Bring to a boil, then reduce the heat to low. Cover the pan partially and cook, stirring occasionally, until thick and rich, about 20 minutes. The chili can be prepared up to 3 days in advance; store in an airtight container in the refrigerator. Rewarm before serving.

Prepare a charcoal or gas grill for direct-heat grilling over medium-high heat. Brush the grill grates clean.

Grill the hot dogs until nicely grill-marked, plump, and warmed through, about 5 minutes. Toast the cut sides of the buns until golden. Alternatively, cook the hot dogs in a pan on the stovetop and toast the buns under the broiler.

To assemble, put a dog in each bun. Top with chili, cheddar, and red onion, and relish these with gusto.

DR. FRANK-N-FURTER'S HOT AND SPICY CHILI DOGS

"YOU'RE A HOT DOG, BUT YOU BETTER NOT TRY TO HURT HER, FRANK FURTER."

ONE-DISH ROCKY RIGATONI
WITH MEATBALLS

In the lead-up to revealing HIS MANLY MASTERPIECE, ROCKY, FRANK-N-FURTER PULLS LEVERS AND MECHANISMS UNTIL ROCKY IS DRAMATICALLY UNVEILED. BAKED MEATBALLS AND TUBULAR RIGATONI MIGHT NOT BE MADE IN A LABORATORY, BUT THIS SCRUMPTIOUS ONE-DISH MEAL IS WORTHY OF A GRAND REVEAL. WHIP UP THESE IRRESISTIBLE MEATBALLS IN ADVANCE, AND STASH THEM IN THE FREEZER FOR UP TO A MONTH FOR A QUICK LAST-MINUTE MEAL, JUST IN CASE A GORGEOUS SOMEONE SHOWS UP WHOM YOU WANT TO SEDUCE.

Makes 6 to 8 servings

Olive oil, for the baking sheet

1 pound ground beef

8 ounces mild Italian pork sausage

¼ cup minced yellow onion

2 large eggs, lightly beaten

½ cup ricotta cheese

½ cup fresh breadcrumbs

1½ teaspoons fine sea salt

1 teaspoon dried oregano, plus more for garnish

½ teaspoon ground fennel

½ teaspoon freshly ground black pepper

1 pound rigatoni

4 cups favorite marinara sauce, warmed

9 ounces shredded mozzarella cheese

¼ cup grated Parmesan cheese

Preheat the oven to 425°F. Generously coat a rimmed baking sheet with olive oil.

In a large bowl, combine the ground beef, sausage, onion, eggs, ricotta, breadcrumbs, salt, oregano, and fennel. Mix gently with your hands until the ingredients are combined evenly. Shape the mixture gently into about 30 meat-balls (about 1 ounce each), then transfer to the prepared baking sheet, spacing the meatballs evenly.

Roast the meatballs, turning once halfway through, until browned, about 20 minutes. Leave the oven on.

While the meatballs cook, make the pasta. Bring a large pot three-fourths full of salted water to a boil over high heat. Add the rigatoni and cook until very al dente, according to the package directions. Drain and return the pasta to the pot.

Add the meatballs, warmed marinara, and about 3 ounces of mozzarella to the pasta and stir gently to combine.

Reduce the oven temperature to 400°F. Coat a 9 by 13-inch baking dish with olive oil.

Transfer the pasta mixture to the prepared baking dish. Top with the remaining 6 ounces of mozzarella and the Parmesan. Bake until golden and bubbly, about 30 minutes.

Let sit for 5 minutes, garnish with a sprinkle of dried oregano, then serve while deliciously hot.

CREATURE OF THE NIGHT
PORK TENDERLOIN

After Janet comes across A TERRIFIED ROCKY IN THE LABORATORY—ON THE HEELS OF SOME EYE-RAISING INDISCRETIONS—SHE SEDUCES THE CREATURE OF THE NIGHT. FRANK, ALONGSIDE RIFF RAFF AND MAGENTA, WITNESSES THE ENTANGLEMENT AND PROMPTLY FAINTS. THIS SEDUCTIVELY TENDER PORK TENDERLOIN, BATHED IN A SWEET-UMAMI SOY AND SESAME MARINADE, IS SO IRRESISTIBLE IT MAY JUST LEAVE YOU WEAK IN THE KNEES.

Makes 4 servings

¼ cup soy sauce

2 tablespoons packed light brown sugar

1 tablespoon Worcestershire sauce

1 tablespoon rice vinegar

1 teaspoon toasted sesame oil

2 garlic cloves, minced

½ teaspoon ground ginger

¼ teaspoon crushed red pepper flakes

1 pound pork tenderloin

Sliced green onions, white and green parts, for garnish

In a small bowl, whisk together the soy sauce, brown sugar, Worcestershire sauce, vinegar, sesame oil, garlic, ginger, and red pepper flakes until the sugar is dissolved. Place the pork in a baking dish and pour the marinade over it, turning the pork to coat it all over. Cover the pork and let marinate in the refrigerator, turning once or twice in the marinade, for 1 to 2 hours. Let come to room temperature for 30 minutes before grilling.

Prepare a charcoal or gas grill for direct- and indirect-heat grilling over medium-high heat. Brush the grill grates clean.

Remove the pork from the marinade, letting any excess drip off. Discard the marinade. Sear the pork over the hottest part of the grill until well browned on all sides, about 5 minutes. Move the pork to the cooler part of the grill, close the grill lid, and continue to cook until the meat is firm to the touch and an instant-read thermometer inserted into the middle of the tenderloin reads 145°F, 13 to 15 minutes longer (for a total of 18 to 20 minutes).

Let the pork rest for 5 to 10 minutes, then slice and serve, garnished with green onions.

RIFF RAFF
RAMEN

Richard O'Brien portrayed the original CHARACTER OF RIFF RAFF, AN OTHERWORLDLY TRANSYLVANIAN WHO, ALONG WITH HIS SISTER MAGENTA, SERVES THE ECCENTRIC AND DEMANDING FRANK-N-FURTER. RIFF RAFF IS TRULY UNFORGETTABLE, MUCH LIKE A BOWL OF FRAGRANT RAMEN. ALTHOUGH AUTHENTIC JAPANESE RAMEN TAKES MANY HOURS (AND SIGNIFICANT CULINARY SKILL), THIS SIMPLIFIED VERSION WITH BRAISED PORK AND A WELL-SEASONED BROTH IS EXCEPTIONALLY DELICIOUS. IF YOU CAN, LOOK FOR FRESH RAMEN NOODLES AT A WELL-STOCKED ASIAN MARKET.

Makes 4 servings

2 pounds boneless pork shoulder, cut into 2 or 3 equal pieces

Fine sea salt and freshly ground black pepper

2 tablespoons neutral oil (such as avocado or canola)

½ yellow onion, roughly chopped

2 garlic cloves, peeled and smashed

1-inch piece fresh ginger, peeled and roughly chopped

6 cups good-quality beef or chicken stock

1 small leek, white and pale green parts, rinsed and chopped

4 ounces shiitake mushrooms, chopped

Soy sauce, sesame oil, and/or chili oil

1 pound fresh or dried ramen noodles

4 large soft-boiled eggs, halved (optional)

2 green onions, white and green parts, sliced

Black and white sesame seeds, for garnish (optional)

Season the pork all over with salt and pepper. In a large Dutch oven or heavy pot over medium-high heat, heat the neutral oil. Add the pork and sear, turning, until nicely browned on two sides, about 6 minutes. Transfer to a plate.

Add the onion and garlic to the Dutch oven and cook, stirring, until the onion starts to brown, about 3 minutes. Add the ginger, stir until it sizzles, then pour in 1 cup of stock and stir, scraping up any browned bits on the bottom of the pot. Add the leek, mushrooms, and the remaining 5 cups of stock. Bring to a boil, then reduce the heat to low. Add the pork and cover the pot. Simmer very gently, turning the pork occasionally, until the pork is fork-tender, 2 to 4 hours. Transfer the pork to a cutting board.

Pour the seasoned stock through a fine-mesh sieve into a large bowl and skim off the fat with a metal spoon; discard the solids. Return the stock to the pot and season with salt, pepper, soy sauce, sesame oil, and/or chili oil to taste. Cover to keep warm.

Cook the ramen noodles according to the package directions. When the pork is cool enough to handle but still warm, break it up into large pieces, discarding any big pieces of fat.

Divide the ramen noodles and pork among bowls. Top each with the warm stock, two egg halves, and garnish wtih green onions and sesame seeds (if it fulfills your desires). Serve.

TRANSYLVANIAN TACOS

Transylvanian Riff Raff proclaims TO FRANK THAT "IT'S ALL OVER, YOUR MISSION IS A FAILURE . . . I'M YOUR NEW COMMANDER, YOU ARE NOW MY PRISONER. WE RETURN TO TRANSYLVANIA." FRANK, ROCKY, AND COLUMBIA ARE KILLED, AND RIFF RAFF ASKS MAGENTA TO ACTIVATE THE TRANSIT CRYSTAL SO THEY CAN BEAM THE DARK CASTLE BACK TO THEIR FARAWAY GALAXY OF TRANSYLVANIA. BEFORE BRAD, JANET, AND DR. SCOTT KNOW WHAT'S HAPPENED, THE CASTLE IS GONE. YOU WON'T HAVE TO TRAVEL QUITE AS FAR AS THE GALAXY OF TRANSYLVANIA TO EAT THESE BRAISED PORK TACOS. SET OUT BOWLS OF ALL YOUR FAVORITE TACO TOPPINGS AND INVITE YOUR FRIENDS TO INDULGE.

Makes 4 servings

BRAISED PORK

2 pounds boneless pork shoulder, cut into 2 or 3 equal pieces

Fine sea salt and freshly ground black pepper

2 tablespoons neutral oil (such as avocado or canola)

½ yellow onion, roughly chopped

2 garlic cloves, peeled and smashed

1 cup Mexican lager-style beer

½ cup fresh orange juice

Juice of ½ lime

2 teaspoons dried oregano

TACO FIXINGS (OPTIONAL)

Small flour or corn tortillas, warmed

Chopped fresh cilantro

Chopped red onion

Crumbled queso fresco

Pickled onions

Pickled jalapeño chiles

Shredded lettuce

Crema or sour cream

To make the pork, season it all over with salt and pepper. In a large Dutch oven or heavy pot over medium-high heat, heat the neutral oil. Add the pork and sear, turning, until nicely browned on two sides, about 6 minutes. Transfer to a plate.

Add the onion and garlic to the Dutch oven and cook, stirring, until the onion starts to brown, about 3 minutes. Pour in the beer and stir, scraping up any browned bits on the bottom of the pot. Stir in the orange juice, lime juice, and oregano and bring to a boil. Add the pork, cover the pot, and reduce the heat to low. Simmer very gently, turning the pork occasionally, until the pork is fork-tender, 2 to 4 hours. Transfer the pork to a cutting board.

Pour the cooking juices through a fine-mesh sieve into a large measuring cup and skim off the fat with a metal spoon. Set aside.

When the pork is cool enough to handle but still warm, use two forks to coarsely shred the pork into bite-size pieces, discarding any big pieces of fat.

Return the pork to the pot and cover to keep warm.

When ready to serve, rewarm the pork in the pot, adding the strained cooking juices to moisten the pork, as needed.

Set out the tortillas, bowls of fixings, and the warm pork and invite guests to build their own tacos, preferably while doing the Time Warp.

I WANT TO BE DIRTY SAUSAGES AND MASH

After Brad and Janet ARE EACH, IN TURN, SEXUALLY LIBERATED BY FRANK—AND THEN FIND OUT ABOUT ONE ANOTHER!—JANET WANTS MORE. SHE AND ROCKY END UP BACK IN THE LABORATORY TOGETHER AND HER FEELINGS RUN WILD: "I'LL PUT UP NO RESISTANCE, I WANT TO STAY THE DISTANCE, I'VE GOT AN ITCH TO SCRATCH, AND I NEED ASSISTANCE." JANET IS BUSTING OUT OF HER COMFORT ZONE AND WANTS TO BE DIRTY. SAUSAGES (AND MASH) ARE ALL ABOUT COMFORT, SO WHEN YOU ARE IN NEED OF SOME, LET THIS CLASSIC DISH FULFILL YOU.

Makes 6 servings

SAUSAGES AND ONION GRAVY

2 tablespoons olive oil,
plus more as needed

6 large, fresh pork sausages
(1½ pounds)

2 tablespoons unsalted butter

1 large yellow onion, halved lengthwise
and thinly sliced crosswise

3 tablespoons all-purpose flour

1½ to 2 cups good-quality beef
or chicken stock

Fine sea salt and freshly ground
black pepper

MASH

3 pounds Yukon gold or yellow
potatoes, peeled and cut into
1-inch chunks

Fine sea salt and ground white pepper

4 tablespoons unsalted butter, at room
temperature, cut into pieces

½ to ¾ cup whole milk, warmed

2 tablespoons minced fresh chives,
plus more for garnish (optional)

To make the sausages and gravy, in a heavy skillet over medium heat, warm 1 tablespoon of olive oil. Add the sausages and cook, turning occasionally, until browned on all sides, about 8 minutes. Transfer to a plate (the sausages will continue to cook in the gravy at the end so it's okay if they aren't fully cooked through).

If the sausages give off enough fat, discard all but 2 tablespoons; otherwise, add the remaining 1 tablespoon of olive oil and the butter to the skillet. Reduce the heat to medium-low and add the onion. Cook, stirring to scrape up any browned bits on the bottom of the pan, and then stirring occasionally, until soft and browned, 18 to 20 minutes. Sprinkle with the flour and cook, stirring, for 1 minute. Slowly pour in 1½ cups

RECIPE CONT'D

of stock, stirring until well combined, then simmer until the gravy thickens slightly, about 3 minutes. Season to taste with salt and pepper. Add more stock, if desired, to get the consistency you like. Transfer the sausages and any of their juices to the skillet, cover, and set aside until the mash is ready.

To make the mash, while the onions are browning, in a large saucepan, combine the potatoes with enough water to cover, then stir in 2 tablespoons of salt. Cover the pan and bring to a boil over high heat. Uncover, reduce the heat to medium, and simmer, stirring occasionally, until the potatoes are tender when pierced with a knife, 15 to 20 minutes. Drain well. Return the potatoes to the pan.

Using a potato masher, roughly mash the potatoes. Scatter the butter over the potatoes and continue to mash. Add enough milk to get the consistency you want. Using a fork, aggressively whip the potatoes back and forth to remove any lumps. Add more milk, as needed, to get the consistency you like. Season with salt and pepper and stir in the chives (if using), then cover the pan to keep warm and set aside.

Return the sausages and gravy to medium-low heat and cook, stirring a few times, until warmed through and the sausages are at least 160°F, or done to your liking.

Serve the sausages and gravy atop the mash, garnished with more chives (if you so desire).

"I'LL PUT UP NO RESISTANCE, I WANT TO STAY THE DISTANCE, I'VE GOT AN ITCH TO SCRATCH, AND I NEED ASSISTANCE."

SHIVER IN ANTICI-PATION SLOW-COOKED THIGH RAGU WITH PASTA

You'll be shivering in antici-pation FOR THIS SLOW-COOKED CHICKEN AND BACON RAGU PASTA. YOU CAN MAKE THIS IN A SLOW COOKER, IF YOU LIKE: JUST ASSEMBLE THE SAUCE AS DIRECTED BUT, BEFORE SIMMERING, TRANSFER THE SAUCE AND THIGHS TO A SLOW COOKER. COVER AND COOK ON LOW HEAT FOR 6 HOURS, THEN PROCEED AS DIRECTED. THIS MAKES MORE SAUCE THAN YOU'LL NEED UNLESS YOU ARE GATHERING A CROWD—SAY, BY ENTICING SOME UNASSUMING GUESTS TO YOUR CASTLE?—BUT YOU CAN FREEZE IT BEAUTIFULLY (FOR UP TO A MONTH), LIKE EDDIE.

Makes 6 servings, with about 11 cups sauce

4 thick-cut bacon slices
(about 5 ounces), diced

1 yellow onion, finely chopped

2 carrots, peeled and finely chopped

2 celery stalks, finely chopped

2 large cloves garlic, minced

Fine sea salt and freshly ground
black pepper

¼ cup tomato paste

½ cup dry red wine

1 (28-ounce) can crushed tomatoes

1 (14-ounce) can diced tomatoes
and their juices

½ cup water

2 teaspoons dried oregano

2 pounds boneless, skinless
chicken thighs

1 pound gemelli, penne,
or fettuccine pasta

Freshly grated Parmesan cheese and
chopped fresh basil, for garnish

In a Dutch oven or large, heavy saucepan over medium heat, cook the bacon, stirring occasionally, until the fat renders and the bacon is golden, about 4 minutes. Using a slotted spoon, transfer the bacon to paper towels to drain. Pour off any excess fat, if you like, but leave at least 1 tablespoon in the pot. Add the onion, carrots, celery, garlic, and 1 teaspoon of salt and cook, stirring occasionally, until the vegetables have softened, about 7 minutes.

Stir in the tomato paste until the vegetables are coated evenly. Pour in the wine and stir, scraping up any browned bits on the bottom of the pot. Add the crushed tomatoes, diced tomatoes and their juices, water, oregano, and 1 teaspoon of pepper and stir to mix well. Bring to a simmer, reduce the heat to low, and cover. Cook, stirring once or twice, for 15 minutes.

Add the chicken thighs, submerging them in the sauce. Bring to a simmer over medium heat, reduce the heat to low, cover the pot, and continue to cook until the chicken is very tender, about 30 minutes. Transfer the chicken thighs to a cutting board. Finely chop the chicken (or use two forks to pull the chicken into shreds). Return the chicken to the sauce along with the reserved bacon, cover, and set over low heat to keep warm while you cook the pasta.

Meanwhile, bring a large pot three-fourths full of salted water to a boil over high heat. Add the pasta and cook until al dente, according to the package directions. Drain and return the pasta to the pot.

Add about 3 cups of sauce to the pasta and toss to coat evenly. Divide the pasta among bowls and top each with more sauce, if you like. Garnish with Parmesan and basil to serve.

Let the remaining sauce cool to room temperature, then transfer it to an airtight container and refrigerate for up to 3 days, or freeze for up to 3 months.

TOUCH-A TOUCH-A TOUCH ME SMOTHERED BREASTS

After Janet gets a taste of "ecstasy [SHE] HAD NEVER DREAMED OF BEFORE . . . HOT BURNING KISSES" FROM FRANK, SHE FINDS OUT BRAD HAS FOUND EQUAL PLEASURE WITH HIM AND SHE ENDS UP IN ROCKY'S ARMS. WITH MAGENTA AND COLUMBIA LOOKING ON, SHE IMPLORES HIM TO "TOUCH-A TOUCH-A TOUCH-A TOUCH ME." THESE SEARED CHICKEN BREASTS, BATHED IN A RICH ONION AND MUSHROOM GRAVY, ARE ECSTASY-PRODUCING. YOU CAN ALSO MAKE THIS WITH THIGHS, JUST LET THEM SIMMER GENTLY IN THE GRAVY A BIT LONGER, UP TO 30 MINUTES.

Makes 4 to 6 servings

4 boneless, skinless chicken breasts (1½ to 2 pounds)

Fine sea salt and freshly ground black pepper

2 tablespoons olive oil

2 tablespoons unsalted butter

1 small yellow onion, halved and thinly sliced

12 ounces cremini or button mushrooms, trimmed and sliced

3 tablespoons all-purpose flour

⅓ cup dry white wine

1¼ cups chicken broth

Mash (page 50) or steamed rice, for serving

Using a meat mallet, lightly pound the chicken to an even ¾-inch thickness and then season the chicken all over with salt and pepper.

In a large, heavy skillet over medium-high heat, warm the olive oil. Add the chicken and cook, turning once, until browned on both sides, about 7 minutes. The chicken will not be cooked through but will finish cooking in the gravy. Transfer the chicken to a plate.

Reduce the heat to medium and add the butter to the skillet to melt. Add the onion and cook, stirring and scraping up any browned bits on the bottom of the skillet, until the onion is browned, 10 to 14 minutes. Reduce the heat if the onion browns too quickly.

Add the mushrooms and continue to cook, stirring until the mushrooms are tender, about 4 minutes. Add the flour, ½ teaspoon of salt, and pepper to taste and stir to coat the vegetables, then slowly pour in the wine and broth. Continue to cook, stirring constantly, until the gravy is smooth, bubbling, and thickens, about 3 minutes.

Return the chicken to the skillet and reduce the heat to low. Cover the skillet and simmer oh-so-gently until the chicken is warm and cooked through, about 5 minutes.

Serve at once, over mash or rice.

THE MAIN EVENT

"Damn it,
Janet,
I love you."

BETTY AND RALF'S WEDDING FRIED RICE

BETTY AND RALF'S
WEDDING FRIED RICE

While attending the wedding OF FORMERLY "PLAIN" BETTY MUNROE—"A WONDERFUL LITTLE COOK"—AND RALF HAPSHATT, JANET CATCHES THE BOUQUET. BRAD PROFESSES HIS LOVE FOR HER: "IF THERE'S ONE FOOL FOR YOU THEN I AM IT. (JANET.) I'VE ONE THING TO SAY AND THAT'S . . . DAMN IT, JANET, I LOVE YOU." TURN PLAIN RICE INTO SOMETHING SPECIAL WITH A MARRIAGE OF CHICKEN, CARROTS, PEAS, GINGER, AND GREEN ONIONS. FEEL FREE TO THROW WHATEVER STRIKES YOUR FANCY INTO THE MIX, LIKE CHOPPED BLANCHED BROCCOLI OR ASPARAGUS, OR EVEN SOME EDIBLE FLOWERS.

Makes 4 to 6 servings

8 ounces boneless, skinless chicken breast, cut into ½- to ¾-inch pieces

Soy sauce or tamari

½ teaspoon toasted sesame oil

Fine sea salt and freshly ground black pepper

1 tablespoon hot water

¼ teaspoon sugar

3 tablespoons neutral oil (such as avocado or canola), plus more as needed

2 large eggs, beaten with a pinch of salt

¼ cup finely chopped yellow onion (about ¼ onion)

1 medium carrot, peeled and diced

½ cup frozen peas

2 garlic cloves, minced

2 teaspoons minced peeled fresh ginger

3 cups cold, leftover cooked rice

2 green onions, white and green parts, thinly sliced

Put the chicken in a medium bowl and toss with 1 teaspoon of soy sauce, the sesame oil, a pinch of salt, and a few grinds of pepper.

In a small bowl, whisk together the hot water, 1 tablespoon of soy sauce, and the sugar. Set aside.

In a large, nonstick skillet or a well-seasoned wok over medium-high heat, heat 1½ teaspoons of neutral oil. Add the eggs and scramble them until cooked through, breaking them into bite-size pieces. Transfer the eggs to a plate.

Add 1 tablespoon of neutral oil to the skillet. When hot, add the chicken and cook, without stirring, until nicely browned on one side, 2 to 3 minutes. Continue to cook, stirring, until just cooked through, about 1 minute longer. Transfer the chicken to a separate plate, leaving any juices or fat in the skillet.

Add another 1½ teaspoons of neutral oil to the skillet. Add the onion, carrot, and a pinch of salt and cook, stirring, until softened, about 4 minutes. Add the peas, garlic, and ginger and cook, stirring, until fragrant and the peas soften, about 1 minute.

Add the remaining 1 tablespoon of neutral oil and the rice. Use a spatula to break up any large chunks of rice. Cook until the rice is warmed through and starts to get a bit toasted, about 4 minutes. If the rice starts to stick, add a bit more oil. Add the sauce mixture, chicken and any juices, and green onions.

Cook, stirring, until warmed through, 2 to 3 minutes. Add the scrambled eggs, stir-fry briefly to bring everything together and warm the eggs. Serve warm.

USHERETTE UMAMI TURKEY BURGERS

Magenta opens the play AS AN USHERETTE, SETTING THE STAGE FOR WHAT'S TO COME "AT THE LATE NIGHT DOUBLE FEATURE PICTURE SHOW." THESE WELL-SEASONED TURKEY BURGERS, TOPPED WITH SOY SAUCE AND BALSAMIC MUSHROOMS, WILL TAKE CENTER STAGE AT YOUR NEXT GATHERING. WORCESTERSHIRE SAUCE IN THE PATTIES GIVE THEM AN EXTRA BOOST OF UMAMI.

Makes 4 burgers

UMAMI MUSHROOMS

1 tablespoon olive oil

5 ounces cremini mushrooms, trimmed and sliced

Fine sea salt and freshly ground black pepper

1 tablespoon soy sauce or tamari

1 teaspoon balsamic vinegar

TURKEY BURGERS

1 pound ground dark-meat turkey

1 large egg, beaten

¼ cup minced yellow onion

2 tablespoons Worcestershire sauce

1 tablespoon country Dijon mustard

½ teaspoon fine sea salt

¼ teaspoon freshly ground black pepper

4 large slices Monterey Jack, cheddar, or other melting cheese (optional)

4 brioche buns or pretzel buns

4 leaves red leaf lettuce, or 1 cup mixed baby lettuces

To make the umami mushrooms, in a skillet over medium-high heat, warm the olive oil. Add the mushrooms, a pinch of salt, and a few grinds of pepper and cook, stirring occasionally, until the mushrooms brown and release their liquid, about 3 minutes. Stir in the soy sauce and vinegar, then transfer the mushrooms to a bowl and cover to keep warm.

Prepare a charcoal or gas grill for direct-heat grilling over medium-high heat. Brush the grill grates clean.

To make the turkey burgers, in a large bowl, combine the ground turkey, egg, onion, Worcestershire sauce, mustard, salt, and pepper. Shape the mixture (it will be quite moist) into four ½-inch-thick patties.

Grill the turkey patties until gorgeously grill-marked and cooked to 165°F, about 5 minutes. Top each patty with a piece of cheese (if using) and cook until melted. Toast the cut sides of the buns until golden.

Serve at once on the toasted buns, topped with the mushrooms and lettuce.

ROCKY'S MUSSELS

With half the brain OF EDDIE, FRANK-N-FURTER CREATES THE "TRULY BEAUTIFUL TO BEHOLD" MUSCLE MAN ROCKY HORROR. WHEN JANET PROCLAIMS THAT SHE DOESN'T "LIKE MEN WITH TOO MANY MUSCLES," FRANK RESPONDS, "I DIDN'T MAKE HIM FOR YOU DEAR. HE CARRIES THE CHARLES ATLAS SEAL OF APPROVAL." MAKE YOUR FANTASIES COME TRUE WITH A BIG PILE OF THESE LUSCIOUS SEA CREATURES. SERVE WITH THE GARLIC TOASTS, OR BE REALLY INDULGENT AND SERVE WITH A HEAPING PILE OF HOT FRIES.

Makes 4 servings

4 thick slices artisan bread

¼ cup extra-virgin olive oil, plus more for brushing

3 garlic cloves, peeled

1 shallot, halved lengthwise and thinly sliced crosswise

Fine sea salt and freshly ground black pepper

4 pounds mussels, scrubbed

1 cup dry white wine

4 tablespoons unsalted butter, at room temperature

2 tablespoons chopped fresh flat-leaf parsley leaves

Preheat the oven to 450°F.

Brush the bread on both sides with olive oil and arrange on a baking sheet. Bake, turning once, until the bread is golden and toasted, about 6 minutes. Lightly rub 1 whole garlic clove over the toasts. Set aside.

In a large, deep pot over medium heat, warm the olive oil. Smash the remaining 2 garlic cloves and add them to the pot along with the shallot. Season with salt and pepper, and cook, stirring occasionally, until the shallot is softened and the mixture is fragrant, about 3 minutes.

Increase the heat to medium-high and add the mussels. Cook, stirring, for 1 minute. Pour in the wine, cover the pot, and steam the mussels until they open, about 5 minutes. Remove the pot from the heat. Discard any mussels that do not open. Using a slotted spoon, transfer the mussels to four wide bowls, dividing them evenly.

Stir the butter into the hot cooking liquid until it melts. Ladle the cooking liquid over the mussels, avoiding any grit on the bottom of the pot. Garnish with parsley, flex your muscles, and serve at once with the toasts.

Dr. Frank-N-Furter might be FROM ANOTHER PLANET, BUT HE'S ALSO A SATIR-
ICAL VERSION OF DR. FRANKENSTEIN, INCLUDING DARINGLY BRINGING HIS OWN CREATION TO
LIFE. HIS EXPERIMENTAL LAB AND HIS ALIEN CREW RESIDE IN A CASTLE THAT, ONE DARK AND
DREARY NIGHT, A NAIVE JANET AND BRAD STUMBLE ACROSS AS THEY SEE A LIGHT, "OVER AT THE
FRANKENSTEIN PLACE." USING CRUNCHY PANKO BREADCRUMBS KEEPS THESE FRIED FISH STICKS
CRISP AND LIGHT. YOU MAY NEVER VENTURE OUT ON A DARK AND DREARY NIGHT TO BUY FROZEN
FISH STICKS AGAIN.

Makes 4 servings

1 pound cod or haddock fillets,
skinned and pinbones removed

Fine sea salt and freshly ground
black pepper

½ cup all-purpose flour

1¼ cups panko breadcrumbs

2 large eggs

Neutral oil (such as canola
or peanut oil), for frying

Tartar sauce, ketchup, and/or
lemon wedges, for serving

Cut the fish into strips about 1 inch
wide and 3 inches long. Season all
over with salt and pepper. Refrigerate, uncovered, for 1 hour.

Place the flour, panko, and eggs
each in a shallow bowl. Whisk the
eggs with ½ teaspoon of salt until
well beaten.

One at a time, coat each fish strip
with flour, shaking off the excess.
Then dip the fish into the egg
mixture, letting the excess drip off.
Finally, dredge the strip in the panko,
pressing to adhere. Transfer to a
baking sheet and repeat with the
remaining fish strips.

In a large, wide skillet over high heat,
warm ½ inch of neutral oil until very
hot. Working in batches, if necessary,
to avoid overcrowding, add the
fish strips to the hot oil in a single
layer so they are not touching. Cook,
turning once, until golden brown and
the fish is cooked through, about
5 minutes total. Transfer to paper
towels to drain.

Serve the fish fingers hot, with
tartar sauce, ketchup, and/or
lemon wedges.

"GREAT SCOTT!" GRILLED SALMON

When Dr. Scott appears AT THE CASTLE, IT IS REVEALED THAT BRAD AND JANET KNOW HIM AND THE ALIEN CREW BECOMES SUSPICIOUS. THEY SOON LEARN THAT HE IS ALSO EDDIE'S UNCLE—"I KNEW HE WAS IN WITH A BAD CROWD, BUT IT WAS WORSE THAN I IMAGINED: ALIENS." THIS MARINATED GRILLED SALMON IS FULL OF ZEST AND LIFE, UNLIKE POOR EDDIE. SERVE IT WITH STEAMED RICE AND GRILLED OR STEAMED VEGGIES.

Makes 4 servings

4 salmon fillets (about 1½ pounds total), pinbones removed

¼ cup reduced-sodium soy sauce, or tamari

2 tablespoons water

Finely grated zest of 1 lemon

Juice of 1 lemon

1 tablespoon packed light brown sugar

½ teaspoon finely grated peeled fresh ginger

Olive oil, for cooking

Sesame seeds, for garnish (optional)

Place the salmon fillets, skin side up, in a baking dish just large enough to hold them. In a small bowl, whisk together the soy sauce, water, lemon zest, lemon juice, brown sugar, and ginger. Pour the marinade over the salmon and refrigerate for at least 30 minutes, or up to 1 hour.

Prepare a charcoal or gas grill for direct-heat grilling over medium heat. Brush the grill grates clean.

Remove the salmon from the marinade, letting any excess drip off. Place the salmon on a plate, pat it dry with paper towels, and rub lightly with olive oil. Pour the marinade into a small saucepan.

Grill the salmon, skin-side down, until just cooked through but still slightly pink in the center, 7 to 10 minutes (depending on how thick the salmon is). Transfer the salmon to a plate.

On the stovetop over medium-high heat, bring the marinade to a boil. Cook for 1 minute. Strain the sauce into a heat-proof bowl.

Divide the salmon among four plates, drizzle the sauce provocatively over the salmon, garnish with sesame seeds (if using), and serve.

SEXY TIME CURRY

Few have embodied the character OF FRANK-N-FURTER MORE SUCCESSFULLY THAN TIM CURRY, WHO PORTRAYED THE SEXY BUT UNHINGED ALIEN IN THE 1973 ORIGINAL LONDON STAGE PRODUCTION AS WELL AS MANY OTHER PRODUCTIONS, INCLUDING THE BLOCKBUSTER FILM ADAPTATION. THIS SEXY VEGETABLE CURRY WILL LEAVE YOU GIDDY WITH PLEASURE BECAUSE IT'S SO DELICIOUS. MAKE SURE TO COOK THE VEGETABLES UNTIL THEY ARE BLISSFULLY TENDER BUT NOT MUSHY.

Makes 6 servings

1 large russet potato (about 1 pound), peeled and cut into ½-inch cubes

Fine sea salt

2 tablespoons neutral oil (such as avocado or canola)

1 medium yellow onion, finely chopped

2 garlic cloves, minced

1 jalapeño or serrano chile, seeded and minced (optional)

2 teaspoons garam masala or pav bhaji masala

1 teaspoon chili powder

1 teaspoon ground cumin

1 teaspoon ground turmeric

1 (14-ounce) can diced tomatoes and their juices

1 (8-ounce) can tomato puree

1 large carrot, peeled and diced

6 ounces green beans, trimmed and chopped crosswise into ¼-inch pieces

2 cups chopped cauliflower florets

4 tablespoons unsalted butter

1 cup boiling water, plus more as needed

¾ cup frozen petite peas

¼ cup chopped fresh cilantro, plus more for garnish

Steamed rice or naan bread, for serving

½ cup finely chopped red onion

1 lime, cut into wedges

In a saucepan, combine the potato with enough water to cover and stir in 1 tablespoon of salt. Bring to a boil over high heat, then reduce the heat to medium and boil gently, stirring occasionally, until the potato pieces are tender but not mushy, about 8 minutes. Drain and set aside.

While the potato cooks, in a skillet with a lid over medium-low heat, warm the neutral oil. Add the yellow onion and cook, stirring, until golden brown, about 8 minutes. Add the garlic and chile (if using) and cook, stirring, for 1 minute. Stir in the garam masala, chili powder, cumin, turmeric, and 1 teaspoon of salt. Add the diced tomatoes and their juices and the tomato puree, increase the heat to medium, and simmer, stirring occasionally, until slightly thickened and fragrant, about 5 minutes.

Add the carrot, green beans, cauliflower, butter, and boiling water and stir to combine. Cover the pan, reduce the heat to low, and cook, stirring occasionally, until the vegetables are tender but not mushy, about 30 minutes.

Add the potato pieces, peas, and cilantro and stir to combine. If the mixture looks dry, add a bit more water. Re-cover the skillet and continue to cook until the vegetables are soft but not mushy, about 10 minutes.

Serve the curry over rice or with naan bread alongside, garnished with cilantro and red onion. Arrange the lime wedges alongside for squeezing suggestively.

DR. SCOTT SPRING VEGGIE STIR-FRY

At the end of the play, DR. SCOTT ENCOURAGES RIFF RAFF TO BLOW FRANK TO OBLIVION WITH HIS LASER BEAM OF ANTI-MATTER. AS DR. SCOTT EXPLAINS TO BRAD, "YOU SAW WHAT HAD BECOME OF EDDIE, SOCIETY MUST BE PROTECTED." BECAUSE HE AND RIFF RAFF SEE EYE TO EYE, THE ALIEN GIVES DR. SCOTT, BRAD, AND JANET A CHANCE TO ESCAPE BEFORE THE ENTIRE HOUSE IS BEAMED BACK TO THE GALAXY OF TRANSYLVANIA. ESCAPE FROM ANOTHER BORING MEAL BY MAKING THIS MIND-BLOWING VEGGIE STIR-FRY. THIS IS JUST A STARTING POINT FOR YOU TO PERSONALIZE WITH YOUR FAVORITE VEGGIES.

Makes 4 servings

¼ cup reduced-sodium soy sauce or tamari

¼ cup water

1 tablespoon sugar

2 teaspoons cornstarch

2 teaspoons grated peeled fresh ginger

2 garlic cloves, minced

¼ teaspoon crushed red pepper flakes, plus more as needed

8 to 10 ounces firm tofu, drained

Fine sea salt and freshly ground black pepper

3 tablespoons neutral oil (such as avocado or canola)

2 medium carrots, peeled and thinly sliced (about 1 cup)

1 bunch thin asparagus (about 12 ounces), tough ends removed, cut into 2-inch-long pieces

6 ounces sugar snap peas, trimmed and halved on the diagonal

3 green onions, white and green parts, sliced

Boiling water, for thinning (optional)

Steamed rice, for serving

In a small bowl, whisk together the soy sauce, water, sugar, cornstarch, ginger, garlic, and red pepper flakes. Set aside.

Cut the tofu block into ¾-inch-thick slabs. Using paper towels, press as much water out of the tofu as possible. Season the tofu with salt and pepper, then cut the slabs into ¾-inch pieces. Set aside.

In a large wok or frying pan over medium-high heat, warm 2 tablespoons of neutral oil. Fry the tofu, turning once, until golden brown on two sides, 3 to 6 minutes. Using a slotted spoon, transfer the tofu to a plate.

Add the remaining 1 tablespoon of neutral oil to the wok. When hot, add the carrots. Cook, stirring often, for 2 minutes. Add the asparagus and cook until the vegetables are crisp-tender, about 2 minutes. Add the sugar snap peas, green onions, and tofu. Reduce the heat to medium and cook, stirring, until the vegetables are warmed through and tender, about 2 minutes. Add the reserved sauce and cook, stirring, until slightly thickened and warmed through, about 1 minute; add a little boiling water, if needed, to thin the sauce to your liking.

Divide the rice among four bowls. Divide the stir-fry among the bowls and serve at once.

EDDIE "DIDN'T LIKE HIS TEDDY" TOSTADAS

Eddie was trouble "from the day HE WAS BORN. WHEN EDDIE SAID HE DIDN'T LIKE HIS TEDDY, YOU KNEW HE WAS A NO GOOD KID." BUT DESPITE HIS UNCLE GIVING UP ON HIM, DR. SCOTT TURNS UP AT THE CASTLE AFTER GETTING A WARNING NOTE FROM EDDIE: "I'M OUT OF MY HEAD. HURRY OR I MAY BE DEAD. THEY MUSTN'T CARRY OUT THEIR EVIL DEEDS." DESPITE HIS PLEA, EDDIE MEETS HIS DEMISE—"SAY A PRAYER FOR EDDIE, I JUST DEFROSTED HIM. HIS DESTINY IS IN THE BAG," FRANK SAYS GLEEFULLY. THESE VEGE-TARIAN BEAN TOSTADAS WILL ROCK AND ROLL YOUR TASTE BUDS.

Makes 4 servings

2 tablespoons neutral oil (such as avocado or canola)

¼ yellow onion, finely chopped

1 garlic clove, minced

½ teaspoon ground cumin

1 cup (about 7 ounces) dried pinto beans, soaked in cold water overnight

4 cups reduced-sodium vegetable broth

Fine sea salt and freshly ground black pepper

Boiling water, as needed (optional)

3 cups finely shredded green cabbage

1 cup finely shredded red cabbage

1 medium carrot, peeled and finely shredded

¼ cup finely chopped fresh cilantro, plus more for garnish

1 lime, halved

8 small corn tostadas, warmed

1 avocado, halved, pitted, peeled, and thinly sliced

In a saucepan over medium-low heat, warm 1 tablespoon of neutral oil. Add the onion and garlic and cook, stirring occasionally, until the onion softens, about 5 minutes. Stir in the cumin. Drain the beans and add them to the saucepan, stirring to combine. Pour in the broth, increase the heat to high, and bring to a boil. Reduce the heat to medium-low and simmer, stirring occasionally, until the beans are very tender but not mushy, about 1 hour (the amount of time it takes depends on the age and size of the beans). Season to taste with salt and pepper. If the beans start to dry out, add a little boiling water; the beans will thicken as they cool.

To make the slaw, in a large bowl, combine the green and red cabbages, and the carrot and cilantro. Drizzle with the remaining 1 tablespoon of neutral oil and squeeze the juice of ½ lime over the top. Season with salt and pepper and toss to combine.

Cut the remaining ½ lime into 4 wedges. Divide the tostadas among four plates. Using a slotted spoon, divide the beans among the tostadas. Top the beans with the slaw, a few slices of avocado, a sprinkle of cilantro, and a wedge of lime, and serve.

"I'M OUT OF MY HEAD. HURRY OR I MAY BE DEAD. THEY MUSTN'T CARRY OUT THEIR EVIL DEEDS."

SASSY

SEXY DRINKS

Make You a Man-hattan

As Frank excitedly unveils his SEXY CREATURE, ROCKY HORROR, HE DESCRIBES HIS PLANS TO ENHANCE ROCKY'S PHYSIQUE USING THE CHARLES ATLAS METHOD—A MUSCLE-BUILDING PROGRAM FROM THE 1920S. THROUGH "DYNAMIC TENSION . . . IN JUST SEVEN DAYS, I CAN MAKE YOU A MAN." THIS CLASSIC WHISKEY COCKTAIL IS EQUALLY SEXY AND DYNAMIC. NOW YOU JUST NEED A HUNKY CREATURE TO SHAKE ONE UP.

Makes 2 cocktails

4 ounces rye whiskey
or bourbon

2 ounces sweet vermouth

4 dashes Angostura bitters
or orange bitters

2 brandied cherries

2 strips orange peel

In a cocktail shaker, combine the whiskey, vermouth, and bitters. Fill the shaker with ice and stir gently with a bar spoon until combined.

Add a few ice cubes to each of two rocks glasses. Strain the cocktail into the glasses, dividing evenly. Garnish each with a brandied cherry and an orange twist, and serve, drinking it all in.

ROSÉ TINT MY WORLD SPRITZ

As each of the main characters PARADES ONTO THE STAGE AS A SLOW-MOTION CHORUS LINE, THEY SHARE THEIR EXPERIENCES WITH FRANK-N-FURTER. "ROSE TINTS MY WORLD KEEPS ME SAFE FROM MY TROUBLE AND PAIN," CLAIMS COLUMBIA—A FAN UNTIL FRANK TOSSED HER ASIDE FOR MUSCLE MAN ROCKY AND KILLED HER LOVER, EDDIE—AND NEWLY "BORN" ROCKY, WHO IS BOTH CONFUSED AND ENJOYING HIS LUSTFUL ADVENTURES. THIS ROSÉ-TINTED COCKTAIL AMPS IT UP WITH A SPLASH OF GIN, TART LEMON JUICE, AND FRESH RASPBERRIES AND IS FULL OF SPARKLE.

Makes 2 drinks

SIMPLE SYRUP

¼ cup water

¼ cup sugar

¼ cup fresh raspberries, plus more for garnish

2 ounces gin

1 ounce fresh lemon juice

1 ounce simple syrup

6 ounces sparkling rosé wine

2 lemon wedges

Sliced fresh strawberries, for garnish

To make the simple syrup, in a small saucepan over medium heat, combine the water and sugar. Simmer, stirring, until the sugar dissolves, about 2 minutes. Pour the syrup into a small glass jar, let cool completely, then cover and refrigerate until chilled, about 2 hours, or set in a bowl placed over an ice bath to chill quickly. Store the remaining syrup in the refrigerator for up to a week.

In a cocktail shaker using a muddler, muddle the raspberries until smashed. Add the gin, lemon juice, and simple syrup. Fill the cocktail shaker with ice, cover, and shake for 10 seconds.

Strain the mixture into two Champagne glasses, dividing evenly. Top each with 3 ounces of sparkling rosé, then garnish each with lemon, strawberry slices, and a few racy raspberries to serve.

TIME WARP BLOOD

ORANGE MARTINI

"Time is fleeting . . ." so don't delay making THESE EXTRA-ORANGE MARTINIS
BECAUSE, BEFORE YOU NOTICE, "MADNESS TAKES ITS TOLL." OF COURSE, IF YOU HAVE TOO MANY OF THESE,
YOU MIGHT ENTER THE TIME WARP, AGAIN. FOR A SWEETER COCKTAIL, USE SWEET VERMOUTH; FOR A MORE
DRY OR LESS SWEET COCKTAIL USE DRY VERMOUTH.

Makes 2 cocktails

4 ounces vodka

4 ounces fresh blood orange juice

1 ounce dry or sweet vermouth

1 ounce orange liqueur, preferably
Cointreau, plus more as needed

4 dashes orange bitters

2 thin blood orange slices,
or 2 strips orange peel

In a cocktail shaker, combine the vodka,
blood orange juice, vermouth, Cointreau
to taste, and orange bitters. Fill the
shaker with ice. Cover and shake gently
until combined.

Strain the cocktail into two martini
glasses, dividing evenly. Garnish each
with a blood orange slice to serve.

DARK AND STORMY

After getting engaged, BRAD AND JANET ARE EN ROUTE TO SEE THEIR EX-TEACHER AND FRIEND DR. EVRETT SCOTT ON A DARK AND STORMY NIGHT. "IT'S TRUE THERE WERE DARK STORM CLOUDS—HEAVY, BLACK, AND PENDULOUS." SEEKING SHELTER AFTER A TIRE BLOWOUT, THEY MAKE FOR THE CASTLE AND THE NIGHT TAKES A DARK AND TWISTED TURN. THE SIMPLICITY OF THIS COCKTAIL BELIES ITS BANG-ON FLAVORS. YOU'RE CERTAIN TO GET THUNDEROUS APPLAUSE WHEN MAKING THESE FOR FRIENDS.

Makes 2 cocktails

4 ounces dark rum, preferably Goslings

1 to 2 ounces fresh lime juice

1 (12-ounce) bottle ginger beer

2 lime wedges

Divide the rum and lime juice evenly to taste between two pint glasses. Stir to combine with a cocktail spoon. Fill the glasses with ice. Top with ginger beer, dividing evenly. Garnish with lime wedges to serve.

SWORD OF DAMOCLES SUNDOWNER

Rocky is born with "A FEELING OF UNAMIABLE DREAD" AS HE LAMENTS THAT "THE SWORD OF DAMOCLES IS HANGING OVER MY HEAD . . . MY LIFE IS A MISERY. I'M AT THE START OF A PRETTY BIG DOWNER." TAKE AWAY THAT FEELING OF DREAD WITH THIS TEQUILA-SPIKED TROPICAL COCKTAIL. IT'S ENOUGH TO GIVE EVEN ROCKY PEACE OF MIND.

Makes 2 cocktails

4 ounces tequila

4 ounces pineapple juice

3 ounces cream of coconut, well shaken

1 ounce fresh orange juice

1 ounce fresh lime juice

2 to 4 dashes orange bitters

2 strips lime peel

In a cocktail shaker, combine the tequila, pineapple juice, cream of coconut, orange juice, lime juice, and orange bitters. Fill the shaker with ice. Cover and shake vigorously until combined.

Fill two rocks glasses with ice. Strain the cocktail into the glasses, dividing evenly. Garnish each with a tart and twisted lime strip to serve.

DRINKING THOSE MOMENTS WHEN THE BLACKNESS WOULD HIT ME. AND THE VOID WOULD BE CALLING.

Good girl Janet is INITIALLY DEMURE—HER "SEX LIFE" WITH BRAD IS LESS SPICY THAN A LOAF OF WHITE BREAD—BUT AFTER SHRUGGING OFF HER MODEST CLOTHES AND BEING SEDUCED BY FRANK SHE GETS AN ITCH TO SCRATCH. AND ROCKY IS HAPPY TO ASSIST. JUST BECAUSE THIS MOCKTAIL IS A VIRGIN DOESN'T MEAN IT'S NOT DELICIOUSLY WILD AND DELIGHTFUL. LET IT THRILL, CHILL, AND FULFILL YOU.

Makes 4 drinks

¼ cup water

¼ cup sugar

1 mint sprig, plus 4 for garnish

Juice of ½ lime

3 cups cold, cubed fresh
seedless watermelon

1 cup lime-flavored sparkling water

4 lime wedges

In a small saucepan over medium heat, whisk together the water and sugar. Add 1 mint sprig. Simmer, stirring, until the sugar dissolves, about 2 minutes. Remove from the heat and stir in the lime juice to combine. Pour the syrup into a small glass jar, let cool completely, then cover and refrigerate until chilled, about 2 hours, or set in a bowl placed over an ice bath to chill quickly.

Place the watermelon in a blender. Remove and discard the mint sprig from the lime simple syrup and add the simple syrup to the blender with the water-melon. Puree on high speed until very smooth. Place a fine-mesh sieve over a bowl and strain the watermelon puree through the sieve.

Fill four pint glasses with ice. Divide the watermelon mixture evenly among the glasses. Top with sparkling water. Garnish each with a macabre mint sprig and lime wedge to serve.

ONCE IN A WHILE
WHITE SANGRIA

When Brad sees Janet WITH ROCKY HE'S CERTAIN "IT'S OVER," DESPITE THE FACT THAT HE'S JUST BEEN WITH FRANK. BRAD LAMENTS, "ONCE IN A WHILE SHE DON'T WANT TO CALL YOU . . . AND ONCE IN YOUR LIFE SHE DON'T WANT TO KNOW YOU . . . YOU LOOK AROUND, THE ONE YOU FOUND, SHE IS GONE." DON'T LET THIS SUMMER SANGRIA GET AWAY. FRESH STRAWBERRIES AND NECTARINES FALL IN LOVE WITH CITRUS, APPLE, AND CRISP WHITE WINE.

Makes 1 pitcher; 4 to 6 servings

2 ounces apple brandy (such as Calvados) or regular brandy, plus more as needed

2 ounces Simple Syrup (page 78), plus more as needed

1 lime, thinly sliced crosswise into rounds

1 orange, thinly sliced crosswise into rounds

1 ripe nectarine, halved, pitted, and thinly sliced

½ green apple, cored and thinly sliced

1 cup sliced fresh strawberries

1 (750-ml) bottle crisp, dry white wine, preferably Spanish wine, chilled

Sparkling water, chilled, to serve

In a large pitcher, stir together the apple brandy and simple syrup to taste. Add the lime, orange, nectarine, apple, and strawberry slices. Pour the white wine over the fruit and stir gently to combine. Taste and add more apple brandy or simple syrup, if you like.

Fill wine glasses with a few cubes of ice each, then fill the glasses about two-thirds full with the sangria, including fruit pieces. Top with sparkling water and serve with a seductive smirk.

SONIC TRANSDUCER "SEND YOU TO ANOTHER PLANET" SHOOTERS

Frank "glues" the cast TO THE STAGE USING HIS SONIC TRANSDUCER, WHICH DR. SCOTT EXPLAINS IS "SOME TYPE OF AUDIO VIBRATORY PHYSIOMOLECULAR TRANSPORT DEVICE . . . A DEVICE THAT IS CAPABLE OF BREAKING DOWN SOLID MATTER AND THEN PROJECTING IT THROUGH SPACE AND, WHO KNOWS, PERHAPS EVEN TIME ITSELF." BASED ON THE MIND ERASER COCKTAIL, THESE SHOOTERS MIGHT JUST SEND YOU TO ANOTHER PLANET . . . JANET.

Makes 2 shooters

2 ounces vodka

2 ounces coffee liqueur, preferably Kahlúa

2 ounces sparkling water or lemon-lime soda (such as 7UP)

In a cocktail shaker, combine the vodka and coffee liqueur. Fill the shaker with ice. Cover and shake gently until well chilled.

Strain the mixture into two large shot glasses, dividing evenly. Pour the sparkling water over the back of a cocktail spoon into each shot glass. Serve.

SASSY SEXY DRINKS

87

DAMMIT JAMMIT

TARTLETS

Uptight Brad asks Janet TO MARRY HIM, IN HIS HEARTFELT (AND DELIBERATELY AWKWARD) BALLAD BEFORE THEIR WHOLE WORLD GOES TOPSY-TURVY. "THE RIVER WAS DEEP BUT I SWAM IT (JANET), THE FUTURE IS OURS SO LET'S PLAN IT (JANET) . . . I'VE ONE THING TO SAY AND THAT'S DAMN IT, JANET, I LOVE YOU." GET READY TO PROFESS YOUR LOVE FOR THESE ADORABLE, SWEET YET TANGY JAM TARTLETS.

Makes 12 tartlets

1 large egg yolk

2 tablespoons whole milk

½ teaspoon pure vanilla extract

1¼ cups all-purpose flour, plus more for dusting

⅓ cup powdered sugar, plus more for dusting (optional)

¼ teaspoon fine sea salt

8 tablespoons (1 stick) cold unsalted butter, cut into small pieces

Cooking spray, for the pan (optional)

¾ cup favorite jam (such as strawberry, raspberry, or sour cherry)

To make the tart dough, in a small bowl, whisk together the egg yolk, milk, and vanilla. In the bowl of a food processor, combine the flour, powdered sugar, and salt. Sprinkle the butter over the top and pulse until the butter breaks up into small pieces. Pour the egg mixture over the flour mixture, then process just until the mixture comes together. Press the dough into a flat disk and wrap it in plastic wrap. Refrigerate for at least 30

minutes, or up to 1 day, before using, or freeze for up to 1 month.

Lightly dust a work surface with flour and roll out the dough on it into a round about ⅛ inch thick. Using a 3¼-inch scalloped or round cutter, cut the dough into rounds. Press together the scraps, re-roll them, and cut the dough into rounds until you have 12 rounds total. Using a 1½-inch star or heart shape, cut out 12 shapes.

Line a 12-cup muffin pan with paper liners and line a small baking sheet with parchment paper. Alternatively, coat the muffin cups with cooking spray and press the pastry directly into the pan, but they can be a bit prudish to come out and play.

Transfer each round to a prepared muffin cup, pressing the dough gently into the bottom and partly up the sides of the cup evenly. Use the tines of a fork to score the bottoms of the tart shells a few times. Arrange the star or heart shapes on the baking sheet. Refrigerate the filled muffin pan and baking sheet for 15 minutes, or cover and freeze for up to 1 month.

Preheat the oven to 350°F.

Fill each tartlet shell with 1 tablespoon of jam, spreading it evenly. Bake the tartlets and shapes until golden brown, about 20 minutes for the tartlets and about 12 minutes for the shapes. Transfer the pans to wire racks and let cool for 20 minutes.

Top tartlets with the baked shapes.

Carefully remove the tartlets from the muffin pan and return the tartlets to the wire rack to cool completely. Dust with powdered sugar (if you are feeling sweet and sensuous) and serve at once.

FRANK'S LABORATORY LEMON BARS

You don't need to "THROW OPEN THE SWITCHES ON THE SONIC OSCILLATOR [OR] STEP THE REACTOR POWER INPUT UP" TO MAKE THESE ETHEREAL LEMON BARS IN YOUR HOME KITCHEN LABORATORY. JUST AVOID ANYONE NAMED FRANK-N-FURTER. THE TENDER SHORTBREAD CRUST AND TART LEMON FILLING CREATE PERFECTION, BUT YOU COULD EXPERIMENT BY SWAPPING KEY LIME JUICE FOR THE LEMON JUICE AND TOPPING THE BARS WITH LASHINGS OF WHIPPED CREAM FOR A KEY LIME PIE VARIATION.

Makes 9 bars

CRUST

8 tablespoons (1 stick) unsalted butter, at cool room temperature, plus more for the pan

1⅓ cups all-purpose flour

¼ cup granulated sugar

¼ teaspoon baking powder

¼ teaspoon fine sea salt

LEMON FILLING

3 large eggs

3 large egg yolks

¾ cup fresh lemon juice

1 cup granulated sugar

6 tablespoons unsalted butter, cut into cubes

Powdered sugar, for dusting

Preheat the oven to 375°F. Lightly coat a 9-inch square baking pan with butter, then line it with parchment paper so two edges come up and slightly over the sides.

To make the crust, in a medium bowl, whisk together the flour, granulated sugar, baking powder, and salt. Using a pastry blender, blend the butter into the dry ingredients until the mixture looks like breadcrumbs. Pour the mixture into the prepared pan and press firmly into an even layer. Bake the crust until golden, about 15 minutes. Using the tines of a fork, poke holes all over the crust (but not all the way through). Set aside on a wire rack.

Reduce the oven temperature to 325°F.

To make the lemon filling, in a saucepan over low to medium-low heat, whisk together the whole eggs, egg yolks, lemon juice, and granulated sugar until well combined. Add the butter. Cook gently, whisking constantly, until the mixture thickens to a soft pudding-like consistency and an instant-read thermometer registers 170°F, about 12 minutes. Pour the lemon filling into the baked crust and smooth into an even layer.

Bake until the filling is just set, about 15 minutes. Let cool on a wire rack for about 30 minutes, then cover the pan and refrigerate until well chilled, at least 3 hours, or up to overnight (the filling will thicken as it cools).

Cut into bars and dust with powdered sugar. Pucker up for a kiss of luscious lemon!

MIDNIGHT DOUBLE

CHOCOLATE FEATURE

BROWNIES

Rocky Horror's "double feature" MASHUP MERGES THE MISADVENTURES OF SPACE ALIENS WITH THE TRAGIC AND WILD PORTRAYAL OF A MAD SCIENTIST. HERE, A DOUBLE DOSE OF CHOCOLATE FEATURES IN THESE DECADENT AND WICKED BROWNIES. IF YOU LIKE, THROW IN 1/2 CUP OF CHOPPED TOASTED WALNUTS OR PECANS WHEN YOU ADD THE CHOCOLATE CHIPS TO THE BATTER.

Makes 18 brownies

Cooking spray, for the baking dish

1 cup (2 sticks) unsalted butter, cut into pieces

1½ cups granulated sugar

¾ cup packed light brown sugar

4 large eggs

1¼ cups unsweetened cocoa powder, sifted (not Dutch process)

1 teaspoon fine sea salt

1 teaspoon baking powder

1 teaspoon baking soda

2 teaspoons pure vanilla extract

1½ cups all-purpose flour

2 cups semisweet chocolate chips

Preheat the oven to 350°F. Lightly coat a 9 by 13-inch baking dish with cooking spray, then line the dish with parchment paper so that two sides come up and over the long edges of the dish.

In a large saucepan over medium heat, melt the butter with the granulated and brown sugars, stirring with a whisk. Once the butter melts, continue to cook, stirring constantly, until the sugar is no longer grainy, about 2 minutes. Remove from the heat.

In a large bowl, whisk together the eggs, cocoa powder, salt, baking powder, baking soda, and vanilla. Scrape the chocolate mixture into the saucepan with the sugar mixture and whisk to combine. Stir in the flour, then stir in the chocolate chips. Scrape the mixture into the prepared baking dish and spread into an even layer.

Bake until just set, 25 to 28 minutes. Transfer to a wire rack and let cool completely.

When cool, lift the brownies out of the dish using the parchment. Cut into 18 equal pieces and serve. The brownies can be stored in an airtight container at room temperature for up to 1 week (as if they'd last that long).

RED LIPS RED VELVET CUPCAKES WITH RED SPARKLE SUGAR

RED LIPS RED VELVET CUPCAKES WITH RED SPARKLE SUGAR

Frank-N-Furter's glossy red lips ARE AS ICONIC AS HIS HIGH HEELS AND FISHNETS. CELEBRATE THOSE BIG RED SMACKERS WITH THESE TENDER RED VELVET CUPCAKES DRAPED WITH A THICK LAYER OF INDULGENT CREAM CHEESE FROSTING. THE LIPS ARE EASILY CUT FROM RED FONDANT, WHICH CAN BE FOUND IN BAKING SUPPLY SHOPS OR ONLINE.

Makes 14 cupcakes

RED VELVET CUPCAKES

2 tablespoons unsweetened cocoa powder, sifted (not Dutch process)

3 tablespoons boiling water

¾ cup buttermilk

4 tablespoons unsalted butter, at room temperature

¼ cup neutral oil (such as avocado or canola)

¾ cup granulated sugar

½ teaspoon fine sea salt

2 large eggs

2 teaspoons pure vanilla extract

1 teaspoon red gel food coloring

1½ cups all-purpose flour

1 teaspoon baking soda

1 teaspoon distilled white vinegar

CREAM CHEESE FROSTING

12 ounces cream cheese, at room temperature

6 tablespoons unsalted butter, at room temperature

1½ cups powdered sugar, sifted

2 teaspoons pure vanilla extract

About 7 ounces red fondant

About 2 tablespoons red sparkle sugar

Preheat the oven to 350°F. Line 14 cups of two standard 12-cup muffin pans with cupcake liners.

To make the cupcakes, sift the cocoa powder into a small bowl and pour the boiling water over it. Whisk to combine, then whisk in the buttermilk.

Using a handheld electric mixer, in a large bowl, beat together the butter, neutral oil, granulated sugar, and salt on medium-high speed until creamy, about 2 minutes. One at a time, add the eggs, beating well after each addition. Beat in the vanilla and food coloring. Add half the flour, beat to combine, then add the buttermilk mixture and beat just until combined. Scrape down the sides of the bowl. Add the remaining flour and mix just until combined. In another small bowl, stir together the baking soda and vinegar, then quickly stir this mixture into the batter. Divide the batter evenly among the prepared muffin cups.

Bake until puffed and a toothpick inserted into the center comes out clean, about 18 minutes. Let cool in the pan on a wire rack for about 5 minutes, then remove the cupcakes from the pan and let cool completely on the rack.

To make the frosting, using a hand-held electric mixer, in a large bowl, beat together the cream cheese and butter on medium-high speed until smooth and fluffy, about 3 minutes. Gradually beat in the powdered sugar and vanilla until thoroughly com-bined, stopping to scrape down the sides of the bowl, as needed. Transfer the frosting to a piping bag fitted with a plain or star tip and pipe the frosting onto the cooled cupcakes.

Roll out the fondant, then cut out 14 lip-shaped pieces. Top each cupcake with fondant lips, then sprinkle with the sparkle sugar. Serve with a kiss.

ROCKY AND FRANK'S
CONFETTI WEDDING
COOKIES

At the end of "I Can Make You a Man," FRANK AND ROCKY WALK ARM AND ARM OUT OF THE LAB (AND INTO THE BEDROOM) TO MUCH GAIETY AND SHOWERS OF CONFETTI CELEBRATING THEIR "NUPTIALS." THROW YOUR RAINBOW CONFETTI SPRINKLES INTO THESE BUTTERY SUGAR COOKIES. A SIMPLE VANILLA GLAZE KEEPS A TIGHT HOLD ON EVEN MORE SPRINKLES, MAKING THESE WORTHY OF ANY FESTIVE OCCASION.

Makes about 2 dozen cookies

CONFETTI COOKIES

1 cup (2 sticks) unsalted butter,
at room temperature

1 cup powdered sugar, sifted

¾ teaspoon fine sea salt

2 teaspoons pure vanilla extract

2 cups all-purpose flour

⅓ cup rainbow sprinkles

GLAZE

½ cup powdered sugar, sifted

1 tablespoon unsalted butter,
at room temperature

1 tablespoon milk

½ teaspoon pure vanilla extract

Rainbow sprinkles, for garnish

Position two oven racks in the upper and lower third of the oven and preheat the oven to 350°F. Line two baking sheets with parchment paper.

To make the cookies, in the bowl of a stand mixer fitted with the paddle attachment, beat the butter, powdered sugar, and salt starting on low speed and increasing to medium-high speed, until well combined and smooth, about 2 minutes. Beat in the vanilla. On low speed, beat in the flour just until the mixture comes together, stopping to scrape down the sides of the bowl, as needed, then stir in the sprinkles.

Scoop up a big tablespoon of dough and roll it into a ball, about 1 inch in diameter. Repeat to use all the dough; you should have about 2 dozen dough balls. Arrange 12 dough balls on each of the prepared baking sheets, spacing them apart. Flatten each cookie gently.

Bake until the cookies are lightly browned around the edges, about 15 minutes, rotating the baking sheets between racks halfway through baking. Let the cookies cool on the baking sheets for 5 minutes, then transfer them to a wire rack to cool completely.

To make the glaze, in a medium bowl and using a handheld electric mixer, beat together the powdered sugar and butter until grainy. Add the milk and vanilla and beat on medium-high speed until very smooth.

Spread the glaze on the cooled cookies and garnish garishly with the sprinkles. Let stand until the glaze is set, about 15 minutes, then serve.

GO BOTH WAYS BLACK AND WHITE COOKIES

With its themes of sexual liberation AND SELF-DISCOVERY, *ROCKY HORROR* HAS REMAINED A FAN FAVORITE FOR DECADES—EVEN THOUGH IT WAS ORIGINALLY CONSIDERED QUITE RISQUÉ (I MEAN, FRANK-N-FURTER SEDUCES EVERYONE). THESE UNENCUMBERED COOKIES, WITH THEIR HALF VANILLA AND HALF CHOCOLATE GLAZES, ARE HAPPILY CONTRASTING YET IN PERFECT SYMMETRY.

Makes 1 dozen cookies

COOKIES

1½ cups all-purpose flour

1 teaspoon baking powder

½ teaspoon baking soda

¼ teaspoon fine sea salt

8 tablespoons (1 stick) unsalted butter, at room temperature

⅔ cup granulated sugar

1 large egg, at room temperature

1 teaspoon pure vanilla extract

⅓ cup sour cream

VANILLA AND CHOCOLATE ICINGS

1½ cups powdered sugar, sifted

2 tablespoons plus 1 teaspoon whole milk, plus more as needed

1 tablespoon light corn syrup

½ teaspoon pure vanilla extract

1 tablespoon Dutch process cocoa powder, sifted

Position two oven racks in the upper and lower third of the oven and preheat the oven to 350°F. Line two large, rimmed baking sheets with parchment paper.

To make the cookies, in a medium bowl, whisk together the flour, baking powder, baking soda, and salt. In the bowl of a stand mixer fitted with the paddle attachment, beat together the butter and granulated sugar on medium-high speed until well combined and creamy, about 1 minute. Beat in the egg and vanilla until smooth. Beat in the sour cream until well combined, then stop to scrape down the sides of the bowl. Add the flour mixture and mix it in on low speed until just combined.

Scoop the dough by the ¼ cup (a cookie scoop works well here) and place on the prepared baking sheets, spacing each dough ball at least 2 inches apart; you should end up with 12 dough balls, 6 per baking sheet.

Bake until the edges are golden brown and the cookies are puffed and cooked through, about 18 minutes, rotating the baking sheets between racks halfway through baking. Let cool on the baking sheet for 5 minutes, then transfer the cookies to a wire rack to cool completely.

To make the icings, in a medium bowl, whisk together the powdered sugar, 2 tablespoons of milk, the corn syrup, and the vanilla until smooth. Transfer

a little less than half of the icing to a small bowl and stir in the cocoa powder and remaining 1 teaspoon of milk until combined. The icings should be thick but easily spreadable; adjust the thickness by adding a little milk to thin, if needed.

Turn the cookies flat side up. Spread the vanilla icing over one half of each cookie, leaving the other half icing-free. Spread the chocolate icing onto the other half. The cookies are best served the day they are made but can be individually wrapped and kept at room temperature for up to 1 week.

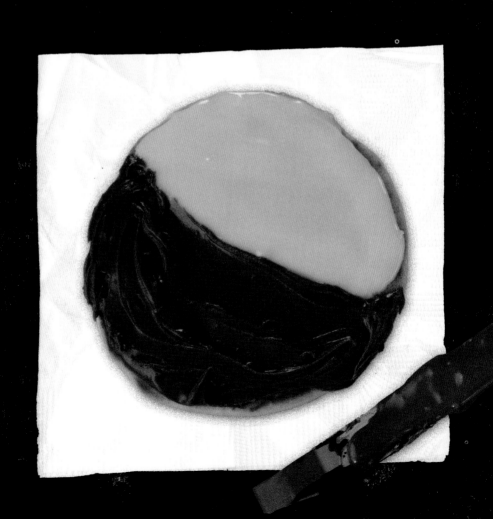

SWEET LOVER BUNS

Frank can really strut HIS STUFF AND SHAKE HIS BUNS IN HIS SKIMPY, SEXY OUTFIT, WHILE BELTING OUT "SWEET TRANSVESTITE" AS A MEANS OF INTRODUCING HIMSELF TO JANET AND BRAD: "DON'T GET STRUNG OUT BY THE WAY THAT I LOOK . . . DON'T JUDGE A BOOK BY ITS COVER. I'M NOT MUCH OF A MAN BY THE LIGHT OF DAY, BUT BY NIGHT I'M ONE HELL OF A LOVER." THESE SOFT, BRIOCHE-LIKE BUNS ARE FILLED WITH SWEET CREAM CHEESE AND CHERRY PIE FILLING. INSTEAD OF MAKING IT FROM SCRATCH, YOU CAN USE CANNED SOUR CHERRY PIE FILLING, OR YOUR FAVORITE JAM OR PRESERVES. (YOU WILL NEED ONLY ABOUT HALF OF THE CHERRY TOPPING; RESERVE THE REST FOR ANOTHER USE OR MAKE ANOTHER BATCH OF DOUGH!)

Makes 6 buns

BUNS

3 tablespoons unsalted butter

½ cup whole milk

¼ cup sugar

1 envelope (2¼ teaspoons) active dry yeast

1 large egg, lightly beaten

2 cups all-purpose flour

½ teaspoon fine sea salt

FILLING

1 (14-ounce) can tart red cherries

6 tablespoons sugar, plus more for sprinkling

1½ tablespoons cornstarch

4 ounces cream cheese, at room temperature

1 teaspoon pure vanilla extract

1 large egg, separated

To make the buns, in a small saucepan over low heat, melt the butter. Stir in the milk and sugar and warm the mixture gently until the sugar dissolves, about 2 minutes. Remove from the heat and pour the mixture into the bowl of a stand mixer. Let cool to between 105°F and 115°F on an instant-read thermometer. Stir in the yeast and let stand until foamy, about 10 minutes.

Stir in the egg, flour, and salt. Attach the dough hook to the mixer and knead the dough on medium speed for about 5 minutes. The dough will be soft and slightly sticky. Form the dough into a ball, cover the bowl with plastic wrap, and let rise in a warm, draft-free spot until very puffy and doubled in size, 1 to 2 hours.

Meanwhile, make the filling. Drain the cherries through a fine-mesh sieve set over a bowl. Measure ⅔ cup of the liquid and pour it into a small saucepan. Add 3 tablespoons of sugar and the cornstarch and whisk to combine. Place the saucepan over medium heat and bring to a simmer, stirring until the mixture is thick and smooth, 2 to 3 minutes. Remove from the heat and stir in the cherries. Set aside to cool.

In a large bowl and using a handheld electric mixer, beat together the cream cheese, remaining 3 tablespoons of sugar, and the vanilla until well combined and smooth. Beat in the egg yolk until well combined. Cover and refrigerate until ready to use.

Line a large, rimmed baking sheet with parchment paper.

Divide the dough into 6 equal pieces, each about 3 ounces. Roll each piece

into a ball, then flatten into a disk. Space the dough disks evenly on the prepared baking sheet. Using a measuring cup, flatten the dough disks so they have a well in the center with a thick rim; they should be about 3½ inches in diameter. Spoon a heaping tablespoon of cream cheese filling into the well of each bun. Cover loosely with plastic wrap and let stand until puffy, about 1 hour.

Position an oven rack in the center of the oven and preheat to 375°F.

Brush the uncovered rims of the dough gently with the egg white and sprinkle with sugar. Top the center of each with a heaping tablespoon of cherry filling.

Bake until the rolls are provocatively puffed and golden, about 18 minutes. Set aside to cool, then devour.

ROCKY (HORROR) ROAD
ICE CREAM SANDWICHES

The studly Rocky Horror MEETS ALMOND- AND MARSHMALLOW-STUDDED ROCKY ROAD ICE CREAM IN THESE SCRUMPTIOUS HUNKY-CHUNKY SANDWICHES. IF YOU LIKE, ONCE THE ICE CREAM SAND-WICHES ARE ASSEMBLED AND HAVE BEEN IN THE FREEZER FOR AT LEAST 30 MINUTES, ROLL THE EDGES IN MINI CHOCOLATE CHIPS, SPRINKLES, OR CHOPPED TOASTED PEANUTS.

Makes 9 or 10 ice cream sandwiches

1¼ cups all-purpose flour,
plus more for dusting

⅓ cup unsweetened cocoa powder
(not Dutch process)

½ teaspoon baking soda

½ teaspoon cream of tartar

¼ teaspoon fine sea salt

8 tablespoons (1 stick) unsalted butter,
at room temperature

1 cup firmly packed dark brown sugar

1 large egg

1 teaspoon pure vanilla extract

2 pints rocky road ice cream

In a large bowl, sift together the flour, cocoa powder, baking soda, cream of tartar, and salt. In another large bowl, and using a handheld electric mixer, beat together the butter and brown sugar on medium-high speed until well combined. Add the egg and vanilla and beat until well combined. Add the flour mixture to the butter mixture and beat on low speed until combined. Press the dough into a disk, wrap it in plastic wrap, and refrigerate for at least 1 hour, or up to 1 day.

Preheat the oven to 350°F. Line two baking sheets with parchment paper.

Lightly dust a work surface with flour and roll out the dough on it into a round about ⅛ inch thick. Using a 3½-inch round or fluted cookie cutter, cut out as many cookies as you can. Transfer the cookies to the prepared baking sheets, spacing them 1 inch apart; with up to 12 cookies on each baking sheet (you should get 18 to 20 cookies total). Press together the scraps, re-roll, and cut out more cookies. Refrigerate the cookies for 15 minutes before baking.

Bake until the cookies puff slightly and look dry on the surface, 7 to 9 minutes. Transfer the baking sheets to wire racks and let the cookies cool on the baking sheets for 15 minutes. Then, using a spatula, transfer the cookies directly to the racks and let cool completely.

Let the ice cream sit at room temperature to soften until just spreadable, about 5 minutes. Place a baking sheet in the freezer.

Turn half of the cookies with bottoms facing up. For each ice cream sandwich, scoop up a heaping ¼ cup of ice cream, then spread it gently into an even thickness on one cookie. Top with a second cookie, bottom side down, press together gently, then transfer to the baking sheet in the freezer. Repeat to make all the ice cream sandwiches. Let freeze until solid, about 1 hour, before serving. The ice cream sandwiches can be individually wrapped and stored in the freezer for up to 2 weeks.

BLOWOUT BAKED CHOCOLATE-GLAZED DONUTS

On their way to visit DR. SCOTT, JANET AND BRAD HAVE A TIRE BLOWOUT ("IT'S TRUE ALSO THAT THE SPARE TIRE THEY WERE CARRYING WAS BADLY IN NEED OF SOME AIR . . . [AND] THEY WERE NOT GOING TO LET A STORM SPOIL THE EVENTS OF THEIR EVENING"). BAKING DONUTS IS INFINITELY EASIER THAN FRYING THEM, OR FIXING A FLAT TIRE, BUT YOU'LL NEED A DONUT-SHAPED PAN TO MAKE THESE. LET THESE DOUBLE CHOCOLATE–GLAZED CAKE DONUTS BLOW YOUR MIND.

Makes 12 donuts

CHOCOLATE DONUTS

Cooking spray, for the pans

1¼ cups all-purpose flour

¼ cup unsweetened cocoa powder (not Dutch process)

¼ cup granulated sugar

¼ cup packed light brown sugar

1 teaspoon baking powder

½ teaspoon baking soda

¼ teaspoon fine sea salt

½ cup whole milk

1 large egg

2 tablespoons neutral oil (such as avocado or canola)

1 teaspoon pure vanilla extract

CHOCOLATE GLAZE

3 tablespoons unsalted butter

1½ cups powdered sugar

3 ounces semisweet chocolate chips

3 tablespoons hot water

1 teaspoon pure vanilla extract

Pinch of fine sea salt

Finely chopped chocolate, for garnish

Preheat the oven to 350°F. Generously coat 12 donut cups (in two 6-cup donut pans) with cooking spray. Set aside.

To make the donuts, in a large bowl, whisk together the flour, cocoa powder, granulated and brown sugars, baking powder, baking soda, and salt.

In a medium bowl, whisk together the milk, egg, neutral oil, and vanilla. Pour the wet ingredients into the dry ingredients and whisk everything until smooth and combined. The batter will be slightly thick. Spoon the batter into a large piping bag fitted with a large plain tip. Pipe the batter into the prepared donut cups, dividing it evenly.

Bake until puffed and cooked through, when a toothpick inserted into a donut comes out clean, 8 to 10 minutes. Let the donuts cool for about 2 minutes, then remove them from the pans and place on a wire rack.

To make the glaze, in a small saucepan over low heat, melt the butter. Add the powdered sugar, chocolate chips, hot water, vanilla, and salt and stir until the chocolate melts and the mixture becomes glossy and smooth. Be careful not to overheat.

While the donuts are still warm, dip the tops lovingly into the chocolate glaze, letting any excess run off. Turn the donuts glazed side up and place on the wire rack. Sprinkle with some of the finely chopped chocolate to garnish. Let set, about 30 minutes. Eat!

"I'M GOING TO GIVE YOU SOME TERRIBLE THRILLS."

PLANET SCHMANET APPLE PIE

Near the end of the play, JANET FEARFULLY ASKS FRANK IF HE IS "GOING TO SEND [THEM] TO ANOTHER PLANET." "PLANET-SCHMANET, JANET," REPLIES AN ANGRY FRANK. "TELL YOU ONCE, WON'T TELL YOU TWICE, YOU'D BETTER WISE UP, JANET WEISS. Y'APPLE PIE DON'T TASTE TOO NICE!" DON'T LET FRANK SCARE YOU, BECAUSE THIS APPLE PIE IS DELIGHTFUL. YOU CAN MAKE THIS WITH A STORE-BOUGHT CRUST RATHER THAN THE HOMEMADE VERSION HERE; JUST PURCHASE TWO 9-INCH ROUNDS, PREFERABLY AN ALL-BUTTER DOUGH.

Makes one 9-inch apple pie; 6 to 8 servings

CRUST

2½ cups all-purpose flour,
plus more for dusting

2 tablespoons sugar

½ teaspoon fine sea salt

12 tablespoons (1½ sticks) cold
unsalted butter, cut into cubes,
plus 2 tablespoons

¾ cup ice-cold water

APPLE FILLING

¾ cup sugar

¾ teaspoon ground cinnamon

¼ teaspoon freshly grated nutmeg

Pinch of fine sea salt

2 tablespoons unsalted butter

3 pounds crisp-tart baking apples
(such as Honeycrisp or Granny
Smith), peeled, cored, and cut into
¾-inch chunks

1½ tablespoons fresh lemon juice

3 tablespoons all-purpose flour

1 teaspoon pure vanilla extract

1 large egg beaten
with 1 teaspoon water

1 tablespoon sugar mixed with
⅛ teaspoon ground cinnamon

Vanilla ice cream or lightly sweetened
whipped cream, for serving

To make the crust, in the bowl of a food processor, blend together the flour, sugar, and salt. Sprinkle the butter pieces over the top and pulse a few times, just until the butter is the size of small peas. Sprinkle the water over the flour mixture, then process just until the mixture starts to come together. Dump the dough into a bowl and press it together. Divide the dough into two disks, cover the bowl, and refrigerate for 30 minutes. The dough can be refrigerated for up to 1 day, or frozen for up to 1 month. Bring the dough to a cool room temperature before rolling it out.

To make the filling, in a small bowl, stir together the sugar, cinnamon, nutmeg, and salt.

In a large skillet over medium heat, melt the butter. Add the apples and lemon juice and stir to combine. Cook, stirring, until the apples just start to release their liquid, about 4 minutes. Sprinkle the sugar mixture over the apples and cook, stirring occasionally, until crisp-tender and the apples have released their liquid, about 3 minutes. Sprinkle the apples with the flour and cook, stirring, until the juices thicken, about 1 minute. Stir in the vanilla. Remove from the heat and spread the apple mixture onto a baking sheet to cool completely.

Position an oven rack in the lower third of the oven and preheat the oven to 400°F.

To roll out the dough, dust a work surface and a rolling pin with flour. Roll out one dough disk on the floured surface into a 12-inch round, about ⅛ inch thick. Roll the dough loosely around the rolling pin and unroll it over a 9-inch pie dish. Roll out the second dough disk into a 12-inch round, about ⅛ inch thick.

Spoon the apple mixture into the pastry shell in an even layer. Lay the second dough round over the top. Trim the top and bottom crusts, leaving a 1-inch overhang. Tuck the dough under itself to create a rim. Use your fingers or a fork to crimp the rim. Place the pie on a baking sheet.

Brush the top and edges of the crust lightly with the egg wash. Sprinkle the top evenly with the cinnamon sugar. Cut a few holes in the top crust for steam vents. Bake the pie until deeply golden brown, 45 to 55 minutes. If the crust starts to get too dark, lay a piece of aluminum foil over the top toward the end of baking.

Let cool to room temperature, about 3 hours. Cut the pie into wedges and serve with a scoop of vanilla ice cream.

TIP: *If you have leftover dough scraps, press them together, roll them out into a long rectangle, brush with melted butter and sprinkle with cinnamon sugar. Roll up like a cinnamon roll, then cut crosswise and bake alongside the pie; they'll take only about 15 minutes.*

SWEET TEMPTATIONS

ACKNOWLEDGMENTS

Taking a deep dive into the *Rocky Horror Show* was a thrillingly fun walk down memory lane. I spent many a midnight feature taking part in the event that is *Rocky Horror* during my early twenties and even my teens (sometimes my parents didn't know about those adventures, ahem). The best thing is the story—whether you get to see the theatrical performance or a late-night showing at the local movie theater—is just as fun now as it was then. In what other musical does the entire audience know all of the lyrics, dress up as the characters, and have an entire subculture devoted to callbacks and audience participation?

One of the most fun parts of doing this book was introducing *Rocky Horror* to my daughter, Poppy, who is herself a theater buff, and has been acting in local musical theater since she was five years old. Thank you, Poppy, for always inspiring me, coming up with fun and crazy recipe ideas, and being willing to try just about anything I cook. A massive thank-you to my husband, Keith Laidlaw, who keeps me laughing even when a recipe test turns disastrous, always fixes the flat tires and spins the best records, and also does most of the dishes. A special thank-you to my dear mom, Ann Crowder, who happily tries all my recipes and helps share the extra food with friends and neighbors. And to my mum-in-law, Pauline Laidlaw, who, when visiting from Scotland, relishes every dessert I develop while also helping with the never-ending dishes.

Thank you to my dear friends (and their kids and partners!), aka my taste testers, always willing to give me feedback, cheer me on, and make sure I don't waste any food: Brittany Ceres, Hannah Eaves, Wendy Goodfriend, Natasha Hauswald, Deanie Hickox, Ingrid Keir, Amanda Lewis, and Noelle Moss. To my neighbors and my husband's coworking colleagues and friends who always accept my platters of food and enjoy them with gusto (cake for breakfast!).

An enormous thank-you to my editor, Randall Lotowycz, who reached out to me to take on this entertaining project and was a joy to work with, and to production editor Melanie Gold, who was always on top of all the details. A big thank-you also to creative director Frances Soo Ping Chow for her beautiful design work, senior publicity manager Seta Zink, senior marketing manager Amy Cianfrone, and everyone at Running Press. And where would we be in all this without Richard O'Brien—thank you for trusting me and giving me the opportunity to work on this cookbook inspired by your masterpiece. It's been truly great to have all your support. Thank you, thank you.

"WHAT'S ON THE SLAB?" RECIPE CONVERSIONS

LIQUIDS

¼ teaspoon	1.25 g/ml	¼ cup	60 g/ml
½ teaspoon	2.5 g/ml	⅓ cup	80 g/ml
1 teaspoon	5 g/ml	½ cup	125 g/ml
1 tablespoon	15 g/ml	1 cup	250 g/ml

WEIGHT

1 oz.	28 g	16 oz. (1 lb.)	454 g
3.5 oz.	100 g	35.3 oz. (2.2 lb.)	1000 g (1 kg)

COMMON INGREDIENTS

VOLUME WEIGHT IN GRAMS

1 cup flour	125 g	1 cup brown sugar, packed	220 g
1 cup granulated sugar	200 g	1 cup butter	225 g
1 cup powdered sugar	120 g	1 stick butter (½ cup)	113 g

OVEN TEMPERATURE

250°F	125°C	350°F	180°C	450°F	230°C
275°F	140°C	375°F	190°C	475°F	250°C
300°F	150°C	400°F	200°C	500°F	260°C
325°F	170°C	425°F	220°C		

INDEX

ABOUT THE AUTHOR

KIM LAIDLAW is a *New York Times* best-selling cookbook author, editor, and recipe developer. She is the author or coauthor of ten cookbooks, including best-sellers *Yellowstone: The Official Dutton Ranch Family Cookbook*, *Tim Burton's The Nightmare Before Christmas* cookbook, *Emily in Paris: The Official Cookbook*, *Five Marys Ranch Raised Cookbook*, *Clueless: The Official Cookbook*, and numerous Williams Sonoma cookbooks. Kim has managed hundreds of cookbook projects, including Kendall-Jackson's *SEASON*, winner of the 2019 IACP Book of the Year Award. Her clients include Disney, Paramount, Netflix, Weber, Hog Island, KitchenAid, American Girl, and more. She is a former professional baker and baking instructor at the San Francisco Cooking School and owns Cast Iron Media, LLC. Kim lives in Petaluma, California, with her Scottish husband, their always-entertaining daughter, and a bountiful home garden.